Radical Notes 5

NEOLIBERALISM, PRIMITIVE ACCUMULATION AND POLITICS IN INDIA

Series Editors

Pratyush Chandra

Pothik Ghosh

Ravi Kumar

Saswat Pattanayak

Radical Notes 5

NEOLIBERALISM, PRIMITIVE ACCUMULATION AND POLITICS IN INDIA

Edited by

Pratyush Chandra

Neoliberalism, Primitive Accumulation and Politics in India
Edited by Pratyush Chandra

First Published, 2011

ISBN 978-93-5002-063-0

Published by
AAKAR BOOKS
28 E Pocket IV, Mayur Vihar Phase I, Delhi 110 091
Phone : 011 2279 5505 Telefax : 011 2279 5641
aakarbooks@gmail.com; www.aakarbooks.com

Printed at
Mudrak, 30 A, Patparganj, Delhi-110 091

A movement in a sense is a struggle over the definition of reality—how reality is constituted. It is this struggle that builds the focus and targets of the movement, informing the praxes towards social transformation. Inherent in this struggle is the act of reclaiming—sense and sensibility, words and meaning.

The word "radical", which in this post-Cold War phase of Global Capitalism or globaloney has been reduced to a general notion characterising all kinds of extremism and deviance, is one such word that has been time and again reclaimed by the practitioners of social transformation. "Radical" derived from the Latin word, 'radix' meaning 'root' = 'basic' = 'fundamental' is a concept that aptly defines a transformatory practice as an endeavour to reveal and target the essence of what is given to us in appearance. Radicalism in this sense is nothing but fundamental transformation rather than politicking in appearances. Further, and foremost, it is the all-round critique of the status quo and its genealogies, rather than accepting the disciplinary divide/boundaries that the capitalist system perpetuates in order to control labour-power and labour, our efforts and their fruits.

Radical Notes is an endeavour to coordinate the radical voices around the globe, with special focus on South Asia. In our view such focus (which could have been anything) is not just for convenience, given the facilitators' cultural and intellectual comfort, but is also needed to concretise any 'radical' pursuit. In our view South Asia provides us the opportunity to visualise the reproduction of 'global' capitalism and struggle against it in a regional setting. But we must remember such focus is always fluid with the ever-dynamic radical needs of the humanity.

Radical Notes booklets are contributions on social, cultural, political or economic issues from counter-hegemonic perspectives, which need not be confined to any established socialist and communist current of thought (though these approaches are most welcome).

Series Editors
Radical Notes

Preface

This collection is not a comprehensive exposition of the concepts of neoliberalism and primitive accumulation. Nor does it claim to be a scientific study of the political economic processes that these concepts connote. It is more a collection of critical analyses of Indian polity that these processes have helped in shaping. Such interventions are never dispassionate and neutral; they frequently take a polemical tone. In fact, they do not shy away from declaring their allegiances to diverse political programmes that obviously derive from the authors' respective understanding of the political economic concepts, processes and situations.

The articles provide a critique of an open instrumentalisation of the Indian state and political forces under neoliberalism. The 'conjunctural appropriation' of political forces of diverse hues and colours to facilitate accumulation – primitive or normal – has been the hallmark of capitalism. The taming of even radical forces (conservative or progressive) for the purpose is not excluded – the design of the state is such that either you break it or you accept a rule or a norm that will bind you to the legitimation needs of the system, keeping you at its service whenever needed.

A major portion of the collection deals with the crisis of the Official Left – how its institutionalisation has increasingly made it an appendage to the needs of the neoliberal capitalist accumulation in various localities, especially in West Bengal, where the left movements have historically been a formidable force. Obviously such institutionalisation is not a linear process – it is not something which is ever complete and without contradictions. In fact, these contradictions must be accounted for in order to envisage any counter-hegemonic realignment.

There are articles where "primitive accumulation" is reclaimed away from its usual historicist reading, which takes it as a one-time-'prehistorical'-event. In this collection, primitive accumulation is understood as a process by which barriers to social reproduction of capital are transcended regularly. Hence, this concept is taken as a key to comprehend anti-capitalism as a network of struggles that hit not just where capital and labour meet regularly to negotiate on the ratio s/v (surplus labour/necessary labour), but also where the conditions are prepared so that such meeting becomes unavoidable.

There are articles that survey the concrete political experience of neoliberalism in India – in terms of political forces, laws and regular 'exceptional' activities of the state, like Operation Green Hunt.

In the end, it must be mentioned that there are arguments in these articles that are limited by the times in which they were written, but this fact perhaps evidences their timeliness.

New Delhi
March 2011

Pratyush Chandra

Contents

1

Singur and the Official Left's Crisis in India

Pratyush Chandra

The Singur events are signs of a crisis borne out of a disjuncture between the Left Front's pragmatic policies and the legacy of the movement and class interests that empowered it. For a long time, the open eruption of this crisis was evaded by the West Bengal government's success in convincing its mass base of its ability to manoeuvre state apparatuses for small, yet continuous gains. It justified all its limitations and inefficacy by condemning the faulty centre-state relationship and a larger conspiracy to destabilise limited reformist gains – for instance, those from reforms in the Bargadari system.

The allegation of conspiracy seemed tangible only to the extent that parliamentary politics drives every opposition party to encash the difficulties incumbent governments face—by peddling popular grievances for advantages in electoral competition. This is the way a representative democracy disperses and defuses challenges to its stability. For illustration, one needs to just review the history of the exit-entry of governments and their economic policies over the past 20 years. There were economic grievances that contributed to the opposition's success in destabilising governments and forming alternative ones, yet there was a remarkable continuity in economic and financial policies. Because of the Indian State's ability to contain popular opposition within the precincts of electoral democracy—the ritual of elections—it could evade any fundamental political economic crisis and did not have to deter from its neoliberal commitments.

Once the Left in West Bengal chose to play by the rules of parliamentary democracy, it faced the continuous threat of defeat in electoral competition. The internalisation of the need to evade this threat transformed its character, thus leading it to aspire beyond being a class party of workers and peasants. It had to become an all people's party—a party that could internalise the dynamo of the status quo, negotiating between diverse, dynamic and antagonistic interests. In other parts of the country too the rise of coalition politics and the possibility of electing representatives decisively regimented the official left's radical rhetoric.

A cosmetic radicalism though is advantageous in the states where it is the incumbent power. It can mobilise its traditional class base, by playing on victimhood, by ritualistic national strikes, etc. The patent logic of the West Bengal government has been that in the absence of a friendly centre, it can do nothing but make the best out of the adverse conditions. Alongside, it has been increasingly using the threat of capital flight to justify its concurrence with the national economic policies.

Behind these usual mechanics of stabilizing its position in the representative democratic set-up resides an essential dilemma or crisis for the official left. The historical legacy of the peasants' and workers' movements that congealed its rule and continue to provide it stability has been both a boon and a bane. This has gravely severed its ability to use traditional means of state coercion for containing its mass base, forcing an informal accommodation or para-legalisation of the Left's traditional mass organisations—their transformation into ideological state apparatuses. Herein lies the danger.

Once these organisations are identified with the officialdom, the grassroots are increasingly alienated and the scope for their independent assertion amplifies. In the history of Bengal's left, this has happened many times—the most formidable one was definitely the Naxalbari movement. Another example was the self-organisation of the Kanoria Jute Mill workers beyond bankrupt bureaucratic trade unionism in the mid-1990s. Singur is the latest case.

One can definitely question the motives of mainstream non-left political parties—like the Congress, Trinamool (TMC) and Bharatiya Janata Party (BJP), which compete with the Left Front to represent the interests of the neo-rich and landed gentry (which includes many absentee landowners) owning bigger portions of land, using 'kishans'—hired labours, bargadars, etc for cultivation. (*EPW*, November 18, 2006) This class, who the West Bengal government claims have consented to land alienation in Singur, joins such movements essentially to obtain various kinds of concessions—a higher price for giving up land to the State and perhaps also for increasing the price for future real estate speculation around the upcoming industrial belt. Moreover, till now the Left Front has succeeded in representing these class interests, which are the main offspring of the limited agrarian and other economic reforms during its rule. But as opportunism is intrinsic to these interests, they are determined to utilise every available mechanism to gain concessions from the regime. Singur is a test case for the official Left's pragmatism —being a local agency for reproducing the general conditions of capitalist accumulation, the Left Front government has to articulate larger neoliberal capitalist designs within the local hegemonic set-up, i.e. it will have to facilitate the representation of local hegemonies within "neoliberal state" apparatuses.

But there is a larger section of the landless, poor peasantry and those frequenting nearby towns for work; for them, the struggles like that of Singur are existential ones. There have been instances of reverse migration also with the closing down of traditional industries. These sections do not possess any faith in neoliberal industrialisation based on flexible, informal and mechanised labour processes. Recently in many parts of the country, these sections of rural poor have been the object and subject of radical mobilisations. It is the fear of their politicisation at the wake of its drive for competitive industrialisation, which is the real worry for the accommodated left in West Bengal, especially the CPM, which has traditionally resisted the mobilisation of the landless in the state, even by its own outfit.

However, the efficacy of capitalist parliamentarianism— the political arrangement suitable for the (post)modern "Eden of the innate rights of man"—lies in reducing class conflicts to lobby politics and competition for representation. Hence, the effective status quoist strategy would be to pose the systemic crisis merely as a temporary crisis of representation. The Left Front and the official opposition in the form of Trinamool and other mainstream parliamentary parties are effectively cooperating in this task. Efforts in this regard include the way the Singur struggle is being projected in corporate media and in political statements—as a Mamata-Buddhadeb tussle or even as manipulation by rival corporate interests, etc. In order to make this strategy vital, the interests (rentier, concessionary or compensational) of local hegemonic classes need to be posed as universal and representative. This could happen only by subjugating the existential, need-based interests of rural poor and proletarians—these interests question the very logic of development within capitalism. Thus their subjugation through within-the-system representation effectively counters whatever counter-hegemonic potential such struggles have. The attempt to reduce the whole struggle to the issues of compensation and other kinds of concessions is part of this strategy. This allows an escape route for both the government and the official opposition—so that symbolic gestures negotiated between these parties can be posed as successes, which can be eventually played as trump cards in electoral competition.

Only the liberation of local struggles from such accommodation can decisively shape the continuity and effectiveness of counter-hegemonic mobilisations and struggles. But this requires radical segments within these struggles not to fall for the cosiness of politics based on vertically homogenised interests, as by default they are hegemonic.

December 29, 2006

2

Neoliberalism and Primitive Accumulation in India: The Need to Go Beyond Capital

Pratyush Chandra and Deepankar Basu

Recent events in Singur—a town which is less than 40 kms away from Kolkata (Calcutta), where the West Bengal government is struggling to acquire and sell 1000 acres of agricultural land to Tata Motors—indicate the extent to which capitalist-parliamentarianism can regiment a counter-hegemonic force once it agrees to play by the rules. At the least, it clearly shows that the Communist government, which boasts of being the longest-running democratically elected Marxist government in the world, is hopelessly caught in the neoliberal project. And Singur is not an isolated event. In the State of West Bengal alone, the process of state-led land grab and the resultant opposition is already gaining momentum in at least three different locations: (a) in Kharagpur, West Medinipur district, where vast tracts of multi-crop farmland are being taken over for yet another Tata vehicle factory; (b) in Nandigram, East Medinipur district, where a chemical industries hub is proposed to be set up by the Salim group on a 10,000-acre area; and (c) in North Bengal where a Videocon Special Economic Zone (SEZ) is proposed to come up in the near future.

Nor is this story limited to West Bengal. Throughout India, resources are being acquired for Special Economic Zones and numerous other industrial schemes meant to facilitate corporate capital expansion. Since laws permitting this acquisitions were passed a year ago, state governments have notified 267 SEZs, which will require more than a half million hectares of land. Of this, the state has already acquired 137,000 hectares for 67 SEZs while another 80 have 'in principle' been approved.[1] The Government has converted the erstwhile Export Processing Zones located at Kandla and Surat (Gujarat), Cochin (Kerala), Santa Cruz (Mumbai-Maharashtra), Falta (West Bengal), Madras (Tamil Nadu), Visakhapatnam (Andhra Pradesh) and Noida (Uttar Pradesh) into SEZs. In addition, three new Special Economic Zones that had been approved for establishment at Indore (Madhya Pradesh), Manikanchan (Salt Lake, Kolkata) and Jaipur have since commenced operations.

In this backdrop, the West Bengal government's adamant attitude towards land acquisition, despite the popular unrest, shows that the Indian State and its agencies, irrespective of their ideological masks, are working relentlessly to provide the private sector with "an internationally competitive and hassle free environment". In this note, we wish to conceptualise this political economic process, identifying its different facets and understanding their interlinkages. It is our contention that the recently re-interpreted Marxist concept of "primitive accumulation" can provide crucial insights in this regard. We wish to demonstrate that current developments in India can be fruitfully understood by employing the notion of primitive accumulation, understood as a constitutive primitive of capitalism, the process which continuously creates and consolidates the capital-relation. Adopting this new perspective might also help in redefining the agenda of struggles and counter-hegemonic politics in the neoliberal context.

Primitive Accumulation: Two Interpretations

As is well known, Marx had brought up the concept of primitive accumulation to try to understand the historical origins of capitalism. It is generally accepted by economic historians that in pre-capitalist modes of production the primary producers (the majority of whom were peasants) had ownership of the means of production, most crucial among them being land. If we agree that capitalism is distinguished from these other modes of production by the relationship of a class of propertyless labourers (who have nothing to sell but their labour power) and a class of propertied capitalists (the owners of the means of production) mediated through the market[2], then the following question naturally arises: how did we arrive at the class of propertyless labourers from a class of producers who had the ownership (or at least the right of usage) of the means of production? It is this historical question that Marx sought to answer with the concept of "primitive accumulation".

In a sense, the answer is already contained in the question. Primitive accumulation is the process by which the producer is divorced from her/his means of production. Since, moreover, land is the primary means of production in pre-capitalist societies, the main focus of primitive accumulation was to separate peasants from the land. While the gradual penetration of market relations had a role to play in this, outright use of force was far more important, and in a sense the key. Only by evicting peasants from their lands and disrupting their livelihood could the development of markets in free labour and land be ensured; and only this could provide the firm basis for the emergence and consolidation of the capital-relation:

> "The capital-relation presupposes a complete separation between the workers and the ownership of the conditions for the realization of their labor. As soon as capitalist production stands on its own feet, it not only maintains this separation, but reproduces it on a constantly extending scale. The process, therefore, which creates the capital-relation, can be nothing other than the process which divorces the worker from the ownership of the conditions of his own labor; it is a process which operates two transformations, whereby the social means of subsistence and production are turned into capital, and the immediate producers are turned into wage-laborers. So-called primitive accumulation, therefore, is nothing else than the historical process of divorcing the producer from the means of production. It appears as 'primitive' because it forms the pre-history of capital, and of the mode of production corresponding to capital."[3]

It is worth recalling that Marx studied the "enclosure movement" in Britain within this overall perspective. One crucial aspect of primitive accumulation should be noted immediately: it effects a redistribution and transfer of *claims* to already existing assets and resources, rather than creating any new assets. In this sense, it is an accumulation of intangible rights and not the accumulation of tangible assets or goods. This aspect of primitive accumulation is important for our purposes because the current frenzy of state-assisted acquisition of land and other resources in India is precisely a process whereby rights of access and usage of already existing resources are being redistributed and transferred.

The last decade has witnessed a resurgence of debate around attempts to re-interpret the concept of primitive accumulation.[4] This debate has indicated that there are two distinct but related interpretations of primitive accumulation, one which stresses the temporal aspect and the other which stresses the constitutive or originary aspect. For the first, more traditional, interpretation the primitiveness of primitive accumulation is understood in a purely temporal sense. Primitive accumulation is seen as the historical phase which created the preconditions for the development of capitalism by forcing the separation of workers and means of production. The second interpretation notes that there is both a temporal and a continuity argument in Marx's account of primitive accumulation. For this interpretation, therefore, the primitiveness of "primitive accumulation" does not arise simply from its location in historical time, relevant only as the initial stage of capitalism; rather, it is the constitutive primitive of the capitalist system, a process that is essential for perpetuating its fundamental class structure—the separation between producers and means of production.

If primitive accumulation is constitutive, then it must arise as a continuous process within capitalism viewed as a global system. Expanded reproduction of the system requires reproduction of the capital-relation at every moment; separation of workers and means of production must be maintained continuously. In its day-to-day functioning, a mature capitalist economy enforces this separation through the market, i.e. by economic means; but at the boundaries (both internal and external), where capitalism encounters other modes of production, property and social relations attuned to those modes and also to the earlier stages of capitalism, other ways of subsistence, primitive accumulation comes into play. More often than not, direct use of force is necessary to effect the separation at the boundaries. And since capitalism, as a global system, continuously encounters other modes of production along with the simultaneity of diverse stages of capitalism in various localities, the constitutive role of primitive accumulation is always in demand. One can probably go so far as to assert that capital accumulation is the extension of primitive accumulation, enforced through the market. In fact, in Volume 3 of *Capital*, Marx himself calls the concentration and centralisation of capital, which occur during the course of market-induced capital accumulation, as "simply the divorce of the conditions of labour from the producers [which occurs through primitive accumulation] raised to a higher power".[5]

But this does not mean that the two are identical. In fact two differences are especially important to grasp for the development of our overall argument:

(a) "[W]hile accumulation relies *primarily* on "the silent compulsion of economic relations [which] sets the seal on the domination of the capitalist over the worker," in the case of primitive accumulation the separation is imposed *primarily* through "[d]irect extra-economic force" (Marx 1867: 899-900), such as the state (Marx 1867: 900), particular sections of social classes (Marx 1867: 879), etc. We can say therefore that primitive accumulation for Marx is a social process instigated by some social actor (the state, particular social classes, etc.) aimed at the people who have some form of direct access to the means of production. This social process often takes the form of a strategy that aims to separate them from the means of production."[6]

(b) "As opposed to accumulation proper, what may be called primitive accumulation... is the historical basis, instead of the historical result, of specifically capitalist

> production' (Marx 1867: 775). While sharing the same principle—*separation*—the two concepts point at two different *conditions* of existence. The latter implies the *ex novo production* of the *separation*, while the former implies the *reproduction*—on a greater scale—of the same *separation*."[7]

Keeping these differences are important because one comes to the rescue of the other when market processes falter. Since capital accumulation operates through the market, the services of primitive accumulation are required almost by definition when the market is in crisis. During crucial phases of capitalist crisis, primitive accumulation emerges to help transcend barriers to accumulation in two ways: (a) by facilitating the transition from the critically fated regime to a new regime of accumulation, and (b) by continuously negotiating the spatial expansion (both internal and external) of capitalism. During periods of transition and expansion, "new enclosures" are required for putting the normal course of capitalist reproduction back on track. Securing these enclosures through force and other "direct extra-economic means" is the function of primitive accumulation. This re-definition allows us to grasp the function of the State and its continuous politico-legal activism in every stage of capitalism.

The present neoliberal phase can probably be understood fruitfully from this perspective. Despite the talk of separating the political from the economic, which is a staple rhetoric of the current phase, it is the state as the instrument of politico-legal repression that facilitates neoliberal expansion. Firstly, the state intervenes with all its might to secure control over resources—both natural and human ("new enclosures")—and secondly, to ensure the non-transgression of the political into the economic, which essentially signifies discounting the politics of labour and the dispossessed from affecting the political economy. David Harvey notes that, "The main substantive achievement of neoliberalisation... has been to redistribute, rather than to generate, wealth and income"; the main mechanisms for achieving this is referred to by Harvey as "accumulation by dispossession", by which he means,

> "... the continuation and proliferation of accumulation practices which Marx had treated of as 'primitive' or 'original' during the rise of capitalism. These include the commodification and privatisation of land and the forceful expulsion of peasant populations...; conversion of various forms of property rights (common, collective, state, etc.) into exclusive private property rights...; suppression of rights to the commons; commodification of labour power and the suppression of alternative (indigenous) forms of production and consumption; colonial, neo-colonial, and imperial processes of appropriation of assets (including natural resources); monetisation of exchange and taxation, particularly of land; the slave trade (which continues particularly in the sex industry); and usury, the national debt and, most devastating of all, the use of the credit system as a radical means of accumulation by dispossession. The state, with its monopoly of violence and definitions of legality, plays a crucial role in both backing and promoting these processes."[8]

Harvey identifies four main features of "accumulation by dispossession": privatisation, commodification, financialisation and the management-manipulation of assets, each feeding on the other, supported by the other and gaining strength from the other. The neoliberal resurgence since the mid-1970s can be understood as capital's counter-revolutionary response to the crisis that enwrapped "embedded liberalism" internationally in the late 1960s, with "signs of a serious crisis of capital accumulation...everywhere apparent. Unemployment and inflation were both surging everywhere, ushering in a global phase of 'stagflation' that lasted throughout much of the 1970s."[9]

The Politics of Primitive Accumulation in India

What is going on in India today can be understood by employing the concept of primitive accumulation (as understood in the second interpretation) in almost all of the above senses: separating primary producers from land; privatisation of the "public", conversion of common property resources into marketable commodities, destroying non-market ways of living, etc. To our mind, each of the instances of ``displacement" or state-led "land grab" are willy-nilly feeding into the overall process of primitive accumulation in India by divorcing primary producers from the land or restricting direct access to other common property resources like forests, lakes, rivers, etc. A question crops up immediately. Being a labour-surplus economy, does India need to generate additional labourers, which is an obvious result of primitive accumulation, before absorbing what is already available? Certainly not, if we think from the perspective of labour. But the answer changes if we see the whole process from the perspective of capital. Fresh entrants into the already burgeoning ranks of the proletariat will increase the relative surplus population—floating, latent and stagnant—depressing real wages and thereby increasing the rates of profits on each unit of invested capital. Moreover, one of the major features of the neoliberal regime of accumulation has been the incessant 'informalisation' of the labour process, and further growth of the relative surplus population makes late-capitalist countries like India finely attuned to this. As Jan Breman notes:

> "Mobilisation of casual labour, hired and fired according to the needs of the moment, and transported for the duration of the job to destinations far distant from the home village, is characteristic of the capitalist regime presently dominating in South Asia."[10]

Separation of producers from their means of production and subsistence, especially land and other natural resources, also creates markets for these resources; and thus comes into being the various agencies that thrive through hucksterage in these markets. These intermediaries play the crucial role of facilitating and normalising the process of primitive accumulation. Examples abound: Trinamool Congress goons, grassroots-level CPI(M) leadership, local middle classes like school teachers, lawyers, and other similar forces in the Singur case; state-traders, local elites-supported Salwa Judum in Chhattisgarh.

The major target of land acquisition in India today is in areas where either peasant movements have achieved some partial success in dealing with capitalist exploitation and expropriation or areas largely inhabited by the indigenous population whose expropriation could not be increasingly intensified because of the welfarist tenor of the pre-liberalisation regime. West Bengal is the prime example of the former, where Left Front rule congealed owing to its constituents' involvement in the popular movements. Now, the movements' institutionalisation and incorporation of the leadership into the state apparatus is facilitating the present-day resurgence of primitive accumulation. Examples of the second kind of area could be parts of Chhattisgarh, Orissa, Andhra Pradesh or Madhya Pradesh, which the corporate sector is eyeing for mining activities and for setting up steel plants.

As an instructive example, if nothing else, let us see how displacement in Singur will affect the various class forces on the ground. While the state apparatuses are trying to secure resources for corporate capital, sections of the local elite, including the affluent farmers led by the mainstream non-left political parties—like the Congress and Trinamool (TMC)—have joined the movement against land acquisition essentially to obtain various kinds of concessions, a higher price for giving up the land to the State and perhaps also for increasing the land price for their future real estate speculation around the upcoming industrial belt. For example, "a TMC leader and ex-pradhan of one of the gram panchayats was initially with the movement, but finally gave away his land. Many of the landed gentry, some of them absentee, who own bigger portions of land, depend on 'kishans' (i.e. hired labours, bargadars, etc) for cultivation of their lands. They principally depend on business or service and have come forward to part with their land in lieu of cash."[11] In case the government talks to the protesters and gives larger concessions, it is these sections that will benefit the most.

The people who are really the backbone of the movement in Singur are the landless working class and poor peasantry. According to a recent report, "many agricultural workers and marginal peasants will lose their land and livelihoods. Though the State Government has decided to compensate the landowners, no policy has been taken for the landless agricultural workers, unrecorded bargadars and other rural households who are indirectly dependent for their livelihood on land and agricultural activities."[12] The region is also inhabited by the poor who "frequent the nearby town, being employed in factories, shops and small businesses. Some of the youth have migrated to cities like Mumbai, Delhi and Bangalore, working there principally as goldsmiths or construction workers. There were several cases of reverse migration when people came back to their village after the closing down of the industries where they were working or finding it more profitable to work on the land than to work in petty industries or businesses, drawing a paltry sum in lieu of hard labour."[13] For this population as also for the landless workers and marginal peasants, the Singur struggles are existential ones.

As an example of the second kind of land acquisition, we can turn our attention to Chhattisgarh. A report on recent developments in Chhattisgarh notes that, in India,

> "[t]ribal lands are the most sought after resources now. Whether it is in Orissa or Chhattisgarh or Andhra Pradesh, if there is a patch of tribal land there is an attempt to acquire it. It is no geographical coincidence that tribal lands are forested, rich with mineral resources (80 per cent of India's minerals and 70 per cent of forests are within tribal areas) and also the site of a sizeable slice of industrial growth. The tribal districts of Chhattisgarh, Orissa, Jharkhand, Karnataka and Maharashtra are the destination of us $85 billion of promised investments, mostly in steel and iron plants, and mining projects. Ironically, these lucrative resources are of no benefit to the local people: an estimate of 10 Naxal-affected states shows that they contribute 51.6 per cent of India's GDP and have 58 per cent of the population. As with Chhattisgarh, all these states have a strong Naxal presence and are witness to movements against land acquisition. The state governments say these protests are Naxal-inspired. Local people say, however, that all they are trying to do is protect their land, forests and livelihood."[14]

Here the State's mode of facilitating primitive accumulation is by raising mercenaries, the Salwa Judum. This extra-legal use of force is supported by the traditional exploiters of the indigenous population—traders, usurers, civil servants and tribal neo-elites, who have functioned as intermediaries in the regime of commerce-based surplus extraction. On the one hand, absence of any recognised land rights of tribal communities, has allowed the State to use principles of *terra nullius* and *eminent domain* to expropriate them. On the other, these communities have continued to exist in defiance of all these legalities. However, with the recent intensification of efforts to secure resources for corporate profiteering, along with the continued presence of primitive extractive modes of exploitation, these communities have been left with no real choices but to arm themselves for securing their unrecognised rights. Hence,

> "Most tribal people living in forests are officially 'encroachers'. They live under the constant threat of being alienated from their land and livelihood. While the government completely failed to reach out to them, the Naxals succeeded in connecting to sections of the people. They spread to the state's 11 districts (200 districts in the country). Unable to contain them, government supported the creation of a civilian militia—Salwa Judum".[15]

Besides these widely discussed cases of recent land acquisition and displacement, there have been numerous conflicts around the rights over water resources over the years. In almost all such cases, the state has come forth as being hell bent upon the construction of big dams and other hydroelectric projects despite all evidence of the net negative marginal costs of these projects. During the past two decades, Narmada Bachao Andolan has been a prominent force constantly exposing the anti-people, anti-environment character of these projects. Even in the Himalayan region of Uttarakhand (site of the legendary Chipko Andolan), riverbeds and surrounding lands have been 'enclosed' for private capital to be used for power generation and lucrative tourism projects. In fact, recent politics in this region cannot be fully understood without understanding the conflicts around these enclosures. Closer to urban India has been the neoliberal systematisation of commercial and financial centres, the `clearing' of slums, in cities like Delhi and Mumbai, which have naturally been the hotbed of the politics of and against "new enclosures".

Understanding all these diverse processes in the framework of primitive accumulation has several strategic implications. Perhaps, most urgently, this can provide a unified framework to locate the numerous struggles going on in the country right from the 'new' social movements, such as landless workers' movements, Narmada Bachao Andolan and other local mobilisations of 'development-victims', to anti-privatisation movements of public sector workers, all the way to the revolutionary movements led by the Maoists. This unified framework can then possibly facilitate dialogue among these movements, something that is more than essential at this juncture if the movement of labour against capital is to be strengthened.

A Future Beyond Capital

Using this framework will also mean re-evaluating many of the theoretical positions that are currently in use. For example, it will be necessary to rethink the classical communist position that characterises the Indian state as semi-feudal and semi-colonial, and thereby sees the struggle of the peasantry as being directed primarily against feudal oppression. It is possible that the inherent limitations of this ideological framework disallow revolutionaries and other radicals to formulate effective strategies against the whole system, a system that preserves various vestigial forms to facilitate accumulation but is not defined by them. Thus, movements struggling against different forms of these vestiges are easily localised, regionalised, marginalised, dispersed, and even used in the intra-ruling class competition and conflicts. The state of the official Indian left is illustrative in this regard. It, too, stresses the presence of "vestiges" and the insufficiency of development, but then turns around and justifies its accommodation in the neoliberal capitalist project as a fight against these vestiges!

Despite the apparent popularity of the new movements of Latin America among the official Left in India, their attachment to a schematic notion of national capitalist development retains all its strength. The devastating consequence, of course, is the deferral of the revolutionary moment till that development is attained; in reality, this amounts to postponing the revolutionary moment beyond the horizon of all concrete possibilities. Surely, this is not simply an ideological problem coming from a faulty understanding of the dynamics of capitalism or socialism. It is a consequence of the official left leadership's accommodation in the capitalist-parliamentary framework, an accommodation moreover that forces them to participate in the competitive race for representation. In the pursuit of presenting itself as the legitimate representative of the "plurality of opinions", which parliamentary politics poses against the notion of class struggle, the left reproduces this plurality within itself, along with its built-in hierarchy. With partial successes in this exercise, representatives of the opinions that count, i.e. the hegemonic class interests, solidify themselves within the party structures. And it is this congealment within the Left Front in West Bengal that leads the "communists" to vocalise neoliberal myths of neutral industrial development, dubbing every protest against its policies as anti-developmental, backward and manipulative. Parallels with the neoliberal demonisation of the transgression of the political into the economic can hardly be missed. Echoing well-heeled mandarins in Delhi, the Left Front government regularly uses the classic threat of capital flight to regiment all protesting voices.

Without comprehending the function of vestiges of earlier modes of production within capitalism or the role of earlier stages of the capitalist mode of production in sustaining capital accumulation, any fundamental challenge to the hegemonic forces in a late capitalist society like India cannot be formulated. It can hardly be denied that, "we suffer not only from the development of capitalist production, but also the incompleteness of that development. Alongside the modern evils, we are oppressed by a whole series of inherited evils, arising from the passive survival of archaic and outmoded modes of production, with their accompanying train of anachronistic social and political relations. We suffer not only from the living, but from the dead. *Le mort saisit le vif* [The dead man clutches onto the living]!"[16]

We will have to recognise the fact that during the stage of imperialism, and more so in the present postcolonial situation, "a high level of capitalist development no longer require[s] the elimination of the traditional class of 'small producers'" and other pre-capitalist 'remnants'.[17] Even in a country like Japan, "in which capitalist society developed only at the so-called finance-capitalist stage of world capitalism, a high level of capitalist development has not been incompatible... with the survival of the traditional class of 'small producers'."[18]

Indian capitalism, like Japanese, came into being in the stage of imperialism, when finance capital and inter-imperialist rivalries were already subjugating the whole world. Moreover, development under direct colonialism foisted some unique features on to the general characteristics of "late capitalism". During the colonial period, "self"-expansion of Indian capital beyond the physical horizons of India was implausible because this would have required an Indian State committed to these interests. Colonialism ruled this out almost axiomatically. However, there were other channels available. The simultaneous existence of various socio-economic formations at diverse levels of Indian society allowed some possibility of 'internal' colonialism and "enclosures", thus, providing the basis for capitalist expansion. Even after Independence, Indian capital relies heavily on the 'diversity' (or unevenness) of Indian economy and society for primitive accumulation and expansion. Additionally, 'semi-feudal' conditions at various locations within the country provide a vast reserve army of labour. The important characteristic of this insecure and docile population is that they can be pulled out of their original locations and thrown into the growing labour market without disturbing the essential fabric of society. In other words, pre-capitalist forms of exploitation provide vast and near permanent pools of cheap labour, which competes with the urban proletariat, thereby bringing the latter under political and economic control. Moreover, this seems[19] to resolve the "agrarian problem" of Indian capitalism, by 'externalising' rural and underdeveloped India from the "core" industrial islands. Concentrating capitalist agricultural development in particular locations of India (for example in west and north-west India), Indian capitalism could afford to under-develop other locations so that they could serve as "external markets" and as reserves of "footloose labour".

Because unevenness is the essential feature of capitalist development, any mode of regulation, including neoliberal globalisation, has to negotiate with diverse stages of societal development. Hence local reactions against this new wave of capitalist consolidation and accumulation are bound to be diverse. The revolutionary vision consists in coordinating these diverse forces for building a formidable challenge to capitalism. Even the struggles against vestigial forms, if they have to be decisive, need to be recognised as contesting capitalist relations that sustain them and are articulated through them. In the Indian context, they are all struggles against a stuttering capitalism, against the inherent brutalities of primitive accumulation. We will have to realise that the movements are not about "saving" tribals/indigenous populations or their way of lives; the movement is a movement of labour against capital. Tribals, poor peasants, marginal peasants, landless labourers, informal sector workers, all these sub-classes are fighting against the tyranny of capital, against being fed—with their labour and resources—into the capitalist machinery. Obviously, in this fight against capital, we cannot cling to any nostalgia for a pristine past, rather our vision must be directed towards the future, a future built on the transcendence of capital, a socialist future rooted in a participatory economy and polity. Only then can the vast majority suffering in the margins of capitalism and toiling under vestigial relations, can make a concerted, decisive effort to end the tyranny of capital.

February 7, 2007

Notes and References

1. Prem Shankar Jha, "Compensation Not Enough", *Daily News & Analysis* (October 2, 2006),http://www.dnaindia.com/report.asp?NewsID=1056324&CatID=19
2. Marx refers to this as the capital-relation.
3. Karl Marx, *Capital Vol. 1*, Penguin Books (1976 [1867]), pp. 874-75.
4. See the contributions in *The Commoner No* 2. (September, 2001), http://www.commoner.org.uk/
5. Karl Marx, *Capital Vol. 3*, Penguin Books (1981 [1894]), pp. 354
6. Massimo De Angelis, "Marx and Primitive Accumulation: The Continuous Character of Capital's "Enclosures",*The Commoner No 2* (September, 2001).
7. Ibid. (Note: *ex novo* is used in the sense of 'original' or 'from scratch').

8. David Harvey, *A Brief History of Neoliberalism*, Oxford (2005), p. 159
9. Ibid, p. 12.
10. Jan Breman, *Footloose Labour: Working in India's Informal Economy*, Cambridge University Press (1996), p. 23.
11. Parthasarthi Banerjee, "Land Acquisition and Peasant Resistance at Singur", *Economic and Political Weekly* (November 18, 2006)
12. Paschim Banga Khet Majoor Samity, "Terror Cannot Suppress Them: People's Resistance to Forced Land Acquisition in Singur", (December 6, 2006).
13. Parthasarthi Banerjee, op cit.
14. "Anti-Naxal Operations: A Cover for Exploiting Tribal People", *Down to Earth Vol 15 No 11* (October 18, 2006).
15. Ibid.
16. Karl Marx, "Preface to the First Edition", *Capital Vol 1*, Penguin (1976 [1867]), p. 91.
17. Kozo Uno, *Principles of Political Economy*, Harvester Press (1980 [1964]), p. xxvii.
18. Ibid, p. 125.
19. Japanese Marxist Kozo Uno stressed that capitalism is incapable of solving the agrarian question. "We can say that it became clear on a world scale that the ability to solve the agrarian question would entail the ability to construct a new society to replace capitalism, and we may regard the League of Nations as having been one such attempt. The solution to this problem, of course, means no more than the external expression of the internal contradictions of capitalism, and cannot occur unless the issue of class relations is solved. In this sense, the failure of the League of Nations was only to be expected." (Quoted in Andrew E. Barshay, *The Social Sciences in Modern Japan: The Marxian and Modernist Traditions*, University of California Press (2004), p. 128).

3

Neoliberal Leninism in India and its Class Character

Pratyush Chandra

"Criticism—the most keen, ruthless and uncompromising criticism—should be directed, not against parliamentarianism or parliamentary activities, but against those leaders who are unable—and still more against those who are unwilling—to use parliamentary elections and the parliamentary rostrum in a revolutionary and communist manner. Only such criticism-combined, of course, with the dismissal of incapable leaders and their replacement by capable ones-will constitute useful and fruitful revolutionary work that will simultaneously train the "leaders" to be worthy of the working class and of all working people, and train the masses to be able properly to understand the political situation and the often very complicated and intricate tasks that spring from that situation."

(V.I. Lenin, *Left-Wing Communism: an Infantile Disorder*, Chapter 7)

1. Lenin and the CPI(M)'s Leninism

The Communist Party of India-Marxist (CPI(M))-led Left Front government in its endeavour to industrialise West Bengal, admittedly within the larger neoliberal framework of the Indian state's economic policies, is ready to scuttle every act of popular vigilance in the manner which Lenin would have called "bureaucratic harassment" of workers-peasants' self-organisation. India's official left position on neoliberal industrialisation and its potentiality to generate employment is very akin to what Lenin characterised "Narodism melted into Liberalism", as the official left "gloss[es] over [the] contradictions [of industrialisation] and try to clamp down the class struggle inherent in it."[1]

In fact, the mass organisations of the official left in West Bengal have for a long time been the main bulwarks of the state government to pre-empt any systematic upsurge of the workers and peasants. They have become increasingly what can be called the ideological state apparatuses to drug the masses and keep them in line. And in this, Leninism has been reduced to an ideology, an apologia for the Left Front's convergence with other mainstream forces on the neoliberal path, giving its "steps backwards" a scriptural validity and promoting an image that in fact this is the path towards revolution—all in the name of consolidation and creating objective conditions for revolution. For justifying their compromises locally in West Bengal, CPI(M) leaders have found handy innumerable quotations from Lenin, and sometimes from Marx too. Contradictory principles and doctrines can easily be derived from their statements, if read as scriptures and taken out of contexts. Hence, as a popular saying in India confirms, *baabaa vaakyam pramaanam*, which loosely means, you can prove anything on the basis of scriptures.

Of course, this can be a variety of Leninism, as there are varieties mushrooming like religious sects, but such was not Lenin. Lenin himself never treated Marx's writings as scriptural for justifying his every tactical move. Furthermore, especially after the defeat of other European revolutions, on many occasions he was prepared to acknowledge Russia's "steps backwards", even during the formulation and implementation of the New Economic Policy. His defence of the independence of working class organisation and power beyond state formation in his attack on Trotsky's advocacy of the regimentation of trade unions was especially for countering the counter-revolutionary potential in the Russian state's "steps backwards" by ever-stronger working class vigilance. Lenin had the courage to say, "We now have a state under which *it is the business of the massively organised proletariat to protect itself*, while we, for our part, must use *these workers' organisations to protect the workers from their state*, and to get them to protect our state. Both forms of protection are achieved through the peculiar interweaving of our state measures and our agreeing or "coalescing" with our trade unions."[2] (emphasis mine)

Such was Lenin even as the leader of the Soviet State, unlike the CPI(M)-led Left Front's leadership, which seeks to stabilise its rule in a tiny part of India, where, it admits, its government can have no sovereignty.

The CPI(M)'s energetic peasant leader Benoy Konar (who rails against Naxal conspiracy in every disturbance in West Bengal), a major stalwart in the present debate on repression and agitation in the state, says, "West Bengal is a federal state in a capitalist feudal country. What its government has done is just a miniscule step compared to what Lenin was forced to do, even after the revolution. If this is what upsets these "true" Marxists so much, we request them to stop living in their imaginations and step into the real world."[3] This logic is very instructive, indeed. It is precisely the case—Lenin could afford to do what he was forced to do because the revolution had taken place. Also, the "steps backwards" were essentially for the sustainability of the state, without changing its basic character—workers-peasants' state, taking the risk of further bureaucratisation and distortion, which he thought the independent assertion of the working class would weed out eventually. If Konar and his gurus are forcing themselves to do the same in a "capitalist feudal country", then it is for whose sustainability—of the "capitalist feudal" state?

2. CPI(M) and its Self-Criticisms

Throughout its thirty years of continuous rule, the West Bengal government's main concern has been to stabilise its local rule within the parameters set by India's state formation, and the hegemonic political economic set-up in the country. It boasts of its successes, but at what cost? The exigencies of the parliamentarist integration reinforced the accommodation and consolidation of a "supra-class" ideology within the communist political habits imbibed during its appendage to the nationalist movement, throughout India in general, and West Bengal in particular. This explains a less radical approach towards land reforms in the region.[4] The CPI-CPI(M)'s role became limited to controlling and policing the radicalisation of its own mass base, as in the 1960s-70s, especially with regard to the Naxal movement. It is interesting to note today how every attempt to form an organisation of the rural proletarians and small peasantry, independent of the rich and middle peasant (who benefited from the movements on tenancy rights and against the Bargadari system) dominated Kisan Sabhas, is systematically repressed by Bengal's state machinery and party.

When the CPI(M) capitulated to electoral politics resorting to tactical measures and strategic sloganeering, because of the so-called popular mandate in its parliamentarist pursuit, militancy became a thing to be repeated only in speeches and slogans as its practice can alienate few votes, precious votes. This is not to say that it was only a subjective transition or a matter of conscious choice, rather, it represented the latent politics of the party leadership's class character. In fact, the only thing lacking was a conscious and consistent opposition within, despite the fact that the party was aware of this from the very beginning. In one of its early documents, it noted:

> "The struggle against revisionism inside the Indian Communist movement will neither be fruitful nor effective unless the alien class orientation and work among the peasantry are completely discarded. No doubt, this is not an easy task, since it is deep-rooted and long-accumulated and also because the bulk of our leading kisan activists come from rich and middle peasant origin, rather than from agricultural labourers and poor peasants. Their class origin, social links and the long training given to them give a reformist ideological-political orientation which is alien to proletarian class point and prevent them from actively working among the agricultural labourers, poor and middle peasants with the zeal and crusading spirit demanded of Communists. Hence the need and urgency to rectify and remould the entire outlook and work of our Party in the kisan movement."[5]

To this P. Sundarayya adds in 1973 (when he was the party's general secretary), "the same old reformist deviation is still persisting in our understanding and practice", which frequently leads to "the repudiation of the Party Programme formulations."[6]

This was all before the concern for stabilising its rule and building social corporatism—"peace", "harmony", etc., in West Bengal became the party's prime agenda. Today, the state government's industrialisation and urbanisation policies express the needs of the neo-rich gentry, a considerable section of which is the class of absentee landowners, dominating the bureaucratic apparatuses and service sector, who legitimately want a share in India's corporate development. When the Kolkata session of the All India Kisan Council held on January 5-6, 2007 asks "the state government to forge ahead on the path of industrialisation based on the success of land reforms and impressive agricultural growth"[7], it is simply expressing the interests of all those who have benefited the most from the success of limited agrarian reforms.

The party is aware that if they alienate these class forces, it will not be possible to remain in power in "a constitutional set-up that is not federal in nature" and which reproduces their ideological hegemony through various identitarian and legal relations influencing the voting pattern of the electorate. As the present party general secretary Prakash Karat, notes:

> "It was clear then as now that the policies implemented by Left-led governments would always be circumscribed by the fact that State power vests with the centre while state governments have very limited powers and resources. This is the reality of a constitutional set-up that is not federal in nature. This understanding was further clarified when Left-led governments began to rule in the three states of West Bengal, Kerala and Tripura for longer periods of time. Within all the constraints and limitations of office, these governments have to take steps to fulfil their commitments to the people and offer relief to the working people. While there are urgent issues before Left-led governments, including those of protecting livelihoods in agriculture, creating jobs by means of industrial development, and improving the quality of people's lives, alternative policies in certain spheres can be implemented only within the constraints imposed by the system."[8]

If this is not the Third Way, the there-is-no-alternative (TINA) syndrome, then one wonders what it can be. Zizek defines the Third Way as "simply *global capitalism with a human face*, that is, an attempt to minimise the human costs of the global capitalist machinery, whose functioning is left undisturbed."[9] It is an old disease that inflicts all social democratic parties, once they start talking about consolidation within the bourgeois framework. Compare:

> "Let no one misunderstand us"; we don't want "to relinquish our party and our programme but in our opinion we shall have enough to do for years to come if we concentrate our whole strength, our entire energies, on the attainment of certain immediate objectives which must in any case be won before there can be any thought of realising more ambitious aspirations."

To this Marx and Engels answered back in 1879:

> "The programme is not to be *relinquished*, but merely *postponed*—for some unspecified period. They accept it—not for themselves in their own lifetime but posthumously, as an heirloom for their children and their children's children. Meanwhile they devote their "whole strength and energies" to all sorts of trifles, tinkering away at the capitalist social order so that at least something should appear to be done without at the same time alarming the bourgeoisie."[10] (emphasis original)

This is the state of a self-acclaimed "revolutionary" party caught up in an existential struggle—"tinkering away at the capitalist social order"! Why not, "the journey towards socialism would begin only after the accomplishment of the task of the bourgeois democratic revolution. If the bourgeois did not join the democratic revolution, it would be easier for the working class to establish its leadership in it which would help in the next stage of socialist revolution."[11] So friends, nothing to worry about, on behalf of the working class, the CPI(M) is actually taking time out for accomplishing the 'democratic revolutionary' tasks. If the working classes—rural and urban—are being forced to shut up, it is all for ensuring their leadership! So, "the programme is not to be *relinquished*, but merely *postponed*—for some unspecified period..."

The CPI(M)'s capitulation to an alien class-ideological orientation is stark in its continuous effort to de-radicalise the left trade union politics. Parallel to Sundarayya's self-criticism, Chief Minister Buddhadeb Bhattacharya too has been time and again indulging in his own variety of self-criticism. His statements are very straightforward, as he seldom minces words in his pandering to corporate interests. In one of his interviews to *The Hindu* (November 16, 2005), he says:

> "We did commit certain wrong things in the past. There were investors really afraid of trade unions here. But things have changed... I am in constant touch with our senior trade union leaders and keep telling them that it is now a different situation. ...I tell [trade union leaders] they must behave. If you do not behave companies will close, you will lose your jobs."[12]

The combination of subjective and objective factors determines the tenor of the official left politics everywhere in India today. So the repression of strikers at the Kanoria jute mill in 1993-94 and Singur/Nandigram incidents are not something unexpected. They are expressions of the Left Front's stable rule in West Bengal for thirty years. These are the imperatives rising from the limitations, about which the Front and CPI(M) never tire to talk, and in which their existential politics is embedded. They do so, as there-is-no-alternative.

3. No "Doublespeak", but the "Narodnik-like Bourgeois" speaks

Unsurprisingly, the CPI(M)'s present general secretary Prakash Karat whom some of us used to admire for his strong positions uncomfortable for the parliamentarian lobbies within the party has come out strongly in defence of the same parliamentarian-ism. His general secretaryship demands that. In India, the days are gone when within these communist parties, a general secretary used to be the voice of a particular programmatic tendency. The designation has been increasingly reduced to a 'post' in the permanent hierarchy, where the post-holder like a civil servant voices whichever tendency dominates in the party.

Prakash Karat accuses the 'left opposition' to the Left Front's industrialisation policies of Narodism, which too is not very surprising. It is one of our standard abuses, along with 'infantile disorder', 'revisionism', etc. However, Karat in his defence really means it, when he says: "The CPI(M) will continue to refute the modern-day Narodniks who claim to champion the cause of the peasantry", as he appends this with a note on the Narodniks.[13]

It seems Karat is ignorant—either he feigns it, or it is real — about Lenin's analysis of Narodism. Lenin's criticism of the Narodnik revolutionaries was mainly centred on their faulty understanding of Russian reality; unlike the Narodniks he saw a slow, but definite evolution of capitalism and capitalist market. He stressed strategising on the basis of this new reality. On the other hand, the Narodniks saw capitalism still simply as a possibility, and thus like true petty bourgeois revolutionaries dreamt of evading the ruthlessness of capitalist accumulation, while often lauding bourgeois freedom and democracy. Lenin in his diatribes obviously underlined the utopianism of this programme, but only on the basis of a critique of the political economy of capitalism in Russia. His fundamental stress was to describe the processes of capitalist accumulation, the ruthlessness of which was compounded by its impurity, its 'incompleteness'. Definitely, an important component of Lenin's programme was embedding the democratic struggle against feudal remnants in the unfolding of the socialist revolution:

> "Thus the red banner of the class-conscious workers means, first, that we support with all our might the peasants' struggle for full freedom and all the land; secondly, it means that *we do not stop at this, but go on further.* We are waging, *besides* the struggle for freedom and land, a fight for socialism. The fight for socialism is a fight against the rule of capital. It is being carried on first and foremost by the wage-workers, who are directly and wholly dependent on capital. As for the small farmers, some of them own capital themselves, and often themselves exploit workers. Hence not all small peasants join the ranks of fighters for socialism; only those do so who resolutely and consciously side with the workers against capital, with public property against private property."[14] (emphasis mine)

Lenin's analysis of capitalism in agriculture showed a growing peasant differentiation. This led him to stress the heterogeneity of the proletarian attitude towards diverse peasant classes. He criticised the populism of the Narodniks and also the liberals who put forward a homogenised notion of "narod" (people). The same notion is found in the Indian official left's attitude towards the peasantry and its assessment of the land reform efforts in the left-ruled states. When it calls upon consolidating the gains from land reforms achieved in a "capitalist feudal" society and pursuing industrialisation on their basis, it consistently evades the question of peasant differentiation. Such evasion is a reflection of the consolidation, within the left leadership, of the hegemonic interests that necessarily rose after the limited land reforms measures. As Sundarayya indicated, this lobby had already congealed within the CPI(M) and been affecting its work in the rural areas, much before it enjoyed the cosiness of the state power. Its consistent success in undermining the rise of the rural proletarians and their organisation in West Bengal is indicative of the strength of this lobby. When Benoy Konar and the All India Kisan Sabha speak for industrialisation based on the gains in agriculture, they speak on the behalf of the rising kulaks and upper middle class in West Bengal who would like to invest and profit on the peripheries and as local agencies of the neoliberal industrialisation—in real estate, in outsourcing and other businesses which are concomitant appendages to the neoliberal expansion.

While differentiating the agrarian programme of the Social Democrats (when the revolutionary Marxists still identified themselves with this name) from that of the liberals, Lenin criticised the latter's "distraught Narodism"—"Narodism melting into Liberalism", which represented the Narodnik-like bourgeoisie, and explained:

> "Firstly, the Social-Democrats want to effect the abolition of the remnants of feudalism (which both programmes directly advance as the aim) *by revolutionary means and with revolutionary determination*, the liberals—*by reformist means* and half-heartedly. Secondly, the Social-Democrats stress that *the system to be purged of the remnants of feudalism is a bourgeois system*; they already now, *in advance, expose all its contradictions, and strive immediately to extend and render more conscious the class struggle that is inherent in this new*

> *system and is already coming to the surface*. The liberals ignore the bourgeois character of the system purged of feudalism, gloss over its contradictions and try to damp down the class struggle inherent in it."[15] (emphasis mine)

Here Lenin clearly states that "distraught Narodism" lies, firstly, in its reformist means, and secondly, in not recognising that the system is already a bourgeois system, hence the basic struggle is against the rule of capital. As Lenin indicated and as it is clear in the case of the CPI(M) in West Bengal, the ideology of "distraught Narodism" is an ideology of the class of Narodnik-like local bourgeoisie, which is necessarily Janus-headed. On the one hand, it feels insecure before its established competitors and their 'bigness', thus consistently calls upon the state to protect its interests. On the other, it is mortified when it feels the presence of its impoverished twin—the growing number of proletarians—as a result of capitalism in agriculture and also due to neoliberal "primitive accumulation". Most dangerous is the faithlessness and weariness that this class of rural and urban proletarians displays towards the neoliberal euphoria—since it has already experienced more than 150 years of ups and downs of capitalist industrialisation, and its increasingly moribund nature. The Bengali political elites' "doublespeak" vocalised by the CPI(M) is actually the reflection of the "Narodnik-like" character of the local bourgeoisie and petty bourgeoisie, torn between the ecstatic possibility of their neoliberal integration, on the one hand, and the rising competition and class struggle, on the other. However, the ideology of homogeneous Bengali interests, along with the "communist" organisations and pretensions come handy in controlling these volatile segments, at least temporarily. It is interesting to note, how the CPI(M) leadership evades recognising the class character of "land reforms", "impressive agricultural growth" and industrialisation as far as possible in its discourse, while overstressing their virtues. It is similar to the discursive habits of the Russian liberals—"distraught Narodniks", which Lenin thus noted, while criticising "Mr L.":

> "Depicting the beneficent effect of the French Revolution on the French peasantry, Mr. L. speaks glowingly of the disappearance

> of famines and the improvement and progress of agriculture; but about the fact that this was bourgeois progress, based on the formation of a "stable" class of agricultural wage-labourers and on chronic pauperism of the mass of the *lower* strata of the peasantry, this Narodnik-like bourgeois, of course, says never a word."[16]

4. Conclusion

When their enthusiasm for neoliberal industrialisation is not well received, as a last resort in defence of the neoliberal policies in West Bengal, our 'vanguards' like Prakash Karat and his associates have a ready apologia that "in a constitutional set-up that is not federal in nature", the left government policies "would always be circumscribed by the fact that State power vests with the centre while state governments have very limited powers and resources." (It does not matter that the CPI(M)'s other leader, Benoy Konar, talks of the same constraints by admitting West Bengal as "a federal state in a capitalist feudal country.")

It is tempting to interpret this demand for more federalism in India as representative of "the demand made in certain circles that local self-governing institutions should also be given the autonomy to borrow and to negotiate investment projects with capitalists, including multinational banks and corporations", as Prabhat Patnaik, a foremost Indian political economist, known for his allegiance to the CPI(M) and who has been lately appointed as Kerala's State Planning Board Vice-Chairman, puts it. He continues, "this will further increase the mismatch in bargaining strength between the capitalists and the state organ engaged in negotiating with them, and will further intensify the competitive struggle among the aspirants for investment... This can have only one possible result which is to raise the scale of social 'bribes' for capitalists' investment. This increase in the scale of social "bribes" is an important feature of neo-liberalism."[17]

Particularly relevant in this regard are the CPI(M) leadership's and the West Bengal government's statements on Singur, in which they consistently fetishise the Left Front's ability to win away the Tata project from a poorer state of Uttarakhand—an example of its competency in 'social bribery'! Chief Minister Buddhadeb Bhattacharya again and again with all his frankness defended his Singur sale to Tata—"We showed them various sites, but they settled for Singur. We could not say no to such a project, otherwise it would have gone to Uttarakhand."[18]

This is symptomatic of the extent to which the official Indian left has re-trained itself in the competitive culture of neoliberal industrialisation. Of course, it does not have any parliamentary stake in Uttarakhand. Or does the party leadership want to entice the Uttarakhand people to choose CPI(M), for its efficiency in negotiating or 'bribing' for neoliberal projects? It is obvious that in order to remain the sole contender of the nationalising and globalising interests of the West Bengal hegemonic classes, the CPI(M) leadership has been giving vent to Bengali parochialism of the local "Narodnik-like bourgeoisie".

February 7, 2007

Notes

1. V.I. Lenin, The Narodnik-Like Bourgeoisie and Distraught Narodism, 1903.http://www.marxists.org.uk/archive/lenin/works/1903/nov/05a.htm
2. V.I. Lenin, The Trade Unions. The Present Situation and Trotsky's Mistakes, 1920.http://www.marx2mao.com/Lenin/TUTM20.html
3. Benoy Konar, Left Front Government and Bengal's Industrialisation, *People's Democracy*, October 08, 2006.http://pd.cpim.org/2006/1008/10082006_benoy%20konar.htm
4. See Dipankar Basu, Political Economy of 'Middleness': Behind Violence in Rural Bengal, *Economic and Political Weekly*, April 21, 2001. http://www.epw.org.in/showArticles.php?root=2001&leaf=04&filename=2411&filetype=pdf
5. P. Sundarayya, *Central Committee Resolution on Certain Agrarian Issues and An Explanatory Note*, CPI(M) Publications, 1973.
6. Ibid.
7. All India Kisan Council, Resolution: Unite to Fight and Defeat All Moves to Stop the Industrialisation of West Bengal, *People's Democracy*, January 14 2007. http://pd.cpim.org/2007/0114/01142007_aiks%20meeting.htm

8. Prakash Karat, "Double-Speak" Charge: Maligning the CPI(M), *People's Democracy,* January 28, 2007.http://pd.cpim.org/2007/0128/01282007_prakash.htm
9. Slavoj Zizek, *The Fragile Absolute,* Verso, 2000, p. 63.
10. Karl Marx and Friedrich Engels, Circular Letter to August Bebel, Wilhelm Liebknecht, Wilhelm Bracke and Others, 1879. http://www.marxists.org/archive/marx/works/1879/09/18.htm
11. Benoy Konar, West Bengal: Rationale For Industrialisation, *People's Democracy,* November 06, 2005.http://pd.cpim.org/2005/1106/11062005_benoy%20kumar.htm
12. *The Hindu* November 16, 2005. http://www.hindu.com/2005/11/16/stories/2005111605361100.htm
13. See (8).
14. V.I. Lenin, The Proletariat and the Peasantry, 1905.http://www2.cddc.vt.edu/marxists//archive/lenin/works/1905/nov/12.htm
15. See (1).
16. Ibid.
17. Prabhat Patnaik, An Aspect of Neoliberalism, *People's Democracy,* December 24, 2006.http://pd.cpim.org/2006/1224/12242006_eco.htm
18. *Frontline,* January 27-February 09, 2007. http://www.frontlineonnet.com/fl2402/stories/20070209002911200.htm

4

Globalisation and Primitive Capital Accumulation

Pranab Kanti Basu

The Myth

There is a wonderful sentiment warming the hearts of global intelligentsia. It is the glorious feeling that we have attained the age of the empire without an emperor, that it is truly the age of globalisation where empire does not imply the exercise of the sovereignty of one state over another. With the triumph of globalised capital the whole world has accepted the economic, moral and ethical supremacy of a homogeneous world order based prominently on individualism and the ethics of the market. The days of fighting the imperialist centre and its camp followers are over. So the proper strategy of the down and out should be to accept the empire and seek to end the discriminatory practices of empire operating to their disadvantage. The workers, for example, who are confined by various laws and regulations within the bounds of a nation state, should demand global citizenship.

This feeling of international fraternity persists among the intellectuals in spite of the genocide being perpetrated by the defenders of the faith, in spite of terrible racial and religious killings all around the world. This faith is understandable. The global intellectuals, the diaspora or the semi-diasporic elements have never been so globally mobile before—the third world intellectuals peddling their differences from the first world and the first world intellectuals peddling their sympathy and patronage are having it good like never before. Perhaps another reason for their rhapsodies about the world order is that with the ascendancy of global capital there has been a homogenisation of ruling cultures like never before. This in turn has led to the homogenisation of curriculum across nations, particularly in the field of higher education. This has opened up the accessibility of the global educator's market— with the attendant magical amounts of forex earnings for the savvy intellectuals.

The Reality

Just a somewhat cautious look at what is happening around shows up the claims of a global order for what it is—a part of the ideological apparatus of global capital. The various versions of this vision reinforce the feeling of inevitability of the order of global capital that has percolated all the capillaries of our existence. Let us note in passing that one of the co-authors of the book that really sold this idea globally (becoming a global best seller in the process) is a member of a communist party (Negri and Hardt, 2000). This is not to ridicule the integrity of the man, but to highlight the fact that the leftists have also quietly conceded the inevitability of the triumph of global capital and hence of the need to think of strategies of coexistence and compromise rather than of counter hegemonic practice and confrontation.

The focus of this article is on thinking of counter hegemonic practices/strategies and also simultaneously thinking of the reasons for the failure of the Marxist parties to think of alternatives.

The Theory

Marx's story of the rise of capitalism belongs to the pantheon of modernist teleological constructs of history. At the end of the route we are left with two fundamental contending classes — the working class and the capitalist class. So either we sign off and say 'this is the end of history', or we construct a vision of the future based on the aspirations of the constructed working class. The problem with the revolutionary vision of the future society (i.e. the latter vision) is that it can only grow out of the capitalist order. Apart from the fact that this entails the espousal of the cause of imposing capitalist development in less developed areas (which is the crux of the problem relating to seizure of agricultural land for the capitalists by the leftist state government in West Bengal) this vision is necessarily based on the acceptance of the self-centred modernity of the capitalist order out of which, only, it can grow through a process of dialectical supercession. Hence it necessarily denigrates community and locality, which, to my mind, must be the fundamental pillars of any future society that can overcome the horrors of the current era of global capitalist domination.

This is not any original idea (even if one has the audacity of subscribing to the notion of originality in this post-modern age). Revolutionaries like Mao, Gramsci, and nearer home Shankar Guha Neogi have propounded this. Clearly their communitarian and locality based visions conflicted with the 'pure' Marxist vision. But they never spelt out their theoretical differences with the Marxist vision of counter hegemonic practice. Perhaps, among other reasons, the need for maintaining class solidarity by leaving the iconic value of Marx undisturbed was an important reason. India also has a rich tradition of rural communitarians like Gandhi and Tagore. I do believe that we should seriously evaluate Gandhi's vision of *Swaraj* and Tagore's vision of *Swadesh* and *Samabay*. Their seminal contributions raise two problems, which require independent evaluation not possible within the span of this enquiry. Gandhi's blindness to the social inequity in the caste system is a fundamental lacuna of his thought that has to be properly evaluated, digging out the limitations that it causes in other areas of his vision. Besides, both Gandhi and Tagore's silence or utopian thought about the relation of the community to the state has to be properly problematised. Though we recognise the significance of the views of the rural communitarians, our entry point is Marx's discussion of capitalism, particularly of primitive capital accumulation (PCA).

Globalisation Primitive Capital Accumulation and Marxism

I had suggested elsewhere (Basu, 2007) that globalisation can be analytically viewed as the era when rent extraction, inevitably relying on PCA, has become the predominant means of extraction of surplus by large capital, which is global. I had suggested that global capital not only extracts rent through acquisition of property rights over land and other natural resources, but it also extracts rent on the basis of acquisition of sole rights to knowledge and markets, and through the imposition of immobility on labour. All these it manages through various international laws and regulations. One could club all these uses of the discriminatory powers derived from the same legal framework that is deemed by the faithful to be non-discriminatory, and so impersonal, under the common theoretical rubric of PCA without violence to the fundamental theoretical propositions of Marx.

This homogeneous treatment of various aspects of surplus extraction by global capital is important because it revalues the role of the state, which had been totally stripped of significance by the myth of empire without emperor. The state is necessary for creating and enforcing the system of laws and regulations that are proper to the extraction of surplus by these means. A hierarchy of states, with the north-south division intact, is also necessary to cook up and impose worldwide the discriminatory systems of property rights and immobilities that are constantly evolving to suit the needs of global capital in the changing social and technological environment. At the same time this homogeneous treatment reduces the significance of space, of territory, and of communities based on these localities. I will here attempt to deconstruct an elementary aspect of PCA—use value—and in the process to explore the specificity of spaces. This will reiterate some of the aspects of the counter hegemonic practices that I had mentioned in my earlier paper and also give it some more depth.

Capital is the agency of transformation of direct heterogeneous social relations between humans into homogeneous relations mediated through commodity exchange. But at the core of the homogenisation/alienation lies the process of commoditisation. Failure to give proper thought to the process of commoditisation closes many counter hegemonic options that are of particular value particularly in the age of globalisation. Though this is not a necessary assumption, the process of PCA as narrated in *Capital* starts from the petty production economic. This comes through clearly in the course of the discussions on the relation between use value and exchange value. There is a very interesting discussion of this issue by Spivak (Spivak, 1987). There she comments that Marx does not apparently realise that the category of use value, which he treats as an originary, natural category, is actually shot through with the unnaturalness of exchange values. This of course conforms to the general tenure of the postmodern critique, whish firmly refuses to admit any pure or natural, precultural category. To us this critique is not important as a species of postmodern themes. Its importance lies in the fact that it indicates, though it does not elaborate, the possibility of locating a lacuna of alienation in the category of use value as it is explicated in *Capital,* rather than limiting the analytical/rhetorical force of alienation to the category of exchange value.

Let us elaborate this position with a textual example. Consider the discussion on the commodity circuits. Before the intervention of money we have the circuit C-C. Let us assume that before exchange takes place the owners of C-C are, respectively, X and Y. As the discussion in *Capital* (Marx, 1954) goes, to X the first C is exchange value while the second is use value. Conversely to Y the first C is use value while the last C is exchange value. The implication that is of fundamental importance is that use value is understood as purely personal or subjective. It has not the burden of cultural or social values. In fact the standard critique of neoclassical theory used to harp on the fact that while the classical economists explained prices in terms of the material, socially determined cost factors, the neoclassical theorists explained prices purely in terms of subjective ahistorical utility. (Dobb, 1973). The question of social determination of use values has sometimes crept in as an eclectic criticism but in a purely negative sense: it has been pointed out, and quite correctly, that utility is not a matter of individual preferences but is managed through propaganda for the benefit of capitalist sales. Our concern is with the positive or unmanageable sense of depending on some common non-individualistic ground. The intervention of capital in this narrative of the circuits of commodities follows only after the introduction of money. Let us briefly trace the sequence.

From C-C we go to C-M-C. Money enters as a repository of exchange value, but only as a vanishing moment. But money does not simply drop out of the circuit. So someone holds it purely as a repository of exchange value. But why should anyone want to hold exchange value? That is C-M-C leads to C-M-C-M.... So we have both C-M-C and M-C-M. What is the objective of the second type of circuit? See when X gives up a 'C' to get another 'C', the act is understandable because what one gives up is qualitatively different from what one acquires. But what about the circuit M-C-M? The 'M' at the beginning and the 'M' at the end are not qualitatively different. So what is the point of this exchange? The answer that Marx provides is that the two Ms are quantitatively different and hence the exchange. So we have the motive of accumulation. M-C-M to M-C-M¢. And M¢>M. But how does that happen in a world where all commodities sell at their values? Where does the excess come from? This brings in capitalist class process with labour power commodity. This is the only part of the inputs purchased by the capitalist that adds more value to the produced goods than its own value. Value of a commodity is the abstract labour required for the production of that commodity. The inputs like raw materials, fuel, etc. have already been produced. So an invariant quantity of abstract or undifferentiated labour has already been embodied in them, which they add to the value of the commodity in whose production they are used. Live or direct labour that is employed, on the other hand, adds more value in the course of its consumption in the process of production than what is required for its own reproduction. In plain terms this means that if a worker works for 8 hours in the factory than the commodities that the worker requires for sustaining this effort require less than 8 hours of labour for their production. This is surplus value, which sources the quantitative addition that leads to M¢ being more than M. so the circuit is represented a M-C-C¢-M¢. C is the value of the inputs purchased including labour power, M is its monetary value, C¢ is the expanded value including surplus value, M¢ is the monetary value of C¢. The intervention of money capital, the birth of the labour power commodity leading to the genesis of surplus value that is appropriated as profit (M¢-M), generates another level of alienation. Let us see the difference in the two levels of differentiation and their implication for our vision of possible counter hegemonic strategies.

The two stages of alienation, as I see it (and which is also implicit in the deconstruction of the category of use value by Spivak) are, first, the stage of commoditisation of product and, second, the stage of alienation of labour power as commodity. Commoditisation necessarily involves the insertion of the category of subjective use value. In plain language this means that commodity exchange implies and is implied by release of production from social or community control on what should be produced and on the distribution of social production. It is only then that the product can appear as a use value to the buyer as an individual. So, in the initial commodity circuit that we have discussed the first 'C' is a use value to Y, not to X; and the second 'C' is a use value to X but not to Y. This is the birth of individuality as opposed to community, which must inevitably, i.e. logically lead to the capitalist mode of production. This would be inconceivable in a social system in which both X and Y are mutually concerned about each other because of a certain social bindings. In this sense Spivak deconstructs the category of use value to show that it too is shot through and through with the guilt of exchange value.

The second stage of alienation has received a lot of attention in Marxist literature. The labourer who has lost possession of all alienable means of production (i.e. all means of production that can be taken away from the labouring person without causing loss of life) is left with the possession of the only inalienable means of production—the power to labour, which is reproduced with each reproduction of the life force of the worker. The labourer is forced to sell labour power for a livelihood. Unlike other commodities the seller of this commodity has to enter the workplace to supply labour power as required by the owner of the factory—the capitalist. So the buyer of labour power commands and the seller obeys. This robs the labourer of the means of realising selfhood in work, which is the differentia of human labour. So the labourer is alienated from his labour.

In my previous treatment of PCA, to which I have already referred, I had not looked critically at the first moment of capital formation, viz. the process of commoditisation. The violation of the community is an essential moment in the development of the capitalist mode of production. Its significance is blurred if one concentrates only on the second moment of PCA, which is highlighted in *Capital*. Once we appreciate the significance of the destruction of community modes of existence for the development of capital a possible counter hegemonic strategy suggests itself. Thinking, producing, living in a community mode can evolve an effective opposition to global capital. This also points to a specificity of space that becomes blurred when one extends the theoretical scope of PCA to understand the entirety of rent extraction by global capital. Space is the field in which the locality is embedded. We are not going into the question of how far it is possible to treat spaces just as geographical territories.

How Things Hang Together

One can try to see how the events that are currently of great concern to all 'liberal and/or left' thinking individuals fit into the scheme of analysis that we have outlined. We will try to build upon that analysis to show that the oppositional forces have to be much more discriminatory in their approach to both the question of who are the friends as well as to the question of what should be a meaningful oppositional strategy. Let us specifically concentrate on what has become the focal point of protest against global capital in India—the seizure of agricultural and forest land for alternate use. This would include all kinds of alternative uses like land for building large dams, SEZs, 'chemical hubs', for realty business and so on.

There are two major issues that come through in what the protestors are saying: that compensation has not been properly evaluated and that those who will lose their land have not been taken into confidence. This, of course, apart from widespread indignation at the reign of terror that has been unleashed on unwilling refugees and protestors by the ruling parties, their henchmen, and the police in the states where such acquisition has met with resistance. The latter can be understood from a purely bourgeois liberal position also. That is, taking account of bourgeois forgetfulness. The story of dispossession of agricultural and forest dependent communities from land is nothing new. This phase of PCA is well documented in *Capital.* In fact the more intelligent supporters of the left front government's policy of land acquisition are delivering learned lectures where they point out the fact that the process of dispossession and consequent impoverishment of the labouring people stretched over a period of more than one and a half centuries in England (and look where England is today!). But once this was completed such obvious state coercion was to be limited to the periphery of capitalist development. So the bourgeois liberal could afford to forget the gory past of capital's 'original' homeland and be critical of the violation of bourgeois rights and legal procedures in the course of land acquisition in India. Violation of the bourgeois legal rights enshrined in law and codes of justice, particularly by the state and those in power, have to be strongly resisted both because they violate the innate right to life and livelihood and also because in the absence of such 'democratic rights' it becomes more difficult to organise for an alternative. But though this resistance is of utmost importance, this cannot constitute any counter hegemonic strategy, per se. That is precisely the reason why political parties that subscribe to the strategy of development under the aegis of global capital find no difficulty in joining such protests in regions where they are not in power. Observe for example the CPI(M) in Orissa or Haryana, as well as the TMC in West Bengal.

From the long-term perspective the questions of 'proper' evaluation of compensation and of participation of the possessors of land in the process of reallocation of land to other uses require serious theoretical consideration if any sustained resistance is to evolve. It is in this context that the images of two moments of alienation become important.

It is worthwhile to remember, as I have pointed out earlier, that the process of PCA is not primitive in the sense of prior in time to capitalist accumulation (Basu, 2007). It is always intertwined with capital's expansion. Capital has to find ways and means of affecting PCA in newer pastures to maintain its capability to expand. For example, it is currently engaged in searching routes to PCA in fields like knowledge, information and even in areas that till recently used to be considered processes that are part and parcel of life process like cultural activities and even the games that people play. Recall that the process of PCA in any new field will involve the two moments of commoditisation and subordination to capital.

The first moment of PCA, viz. commoditisation is also the first moment of alienation in the sense of severance of community linkages. This provides the key to understanding the controversy over what constitutes 'proper compensation'. When use values are not just subjective but conditioned by community norms, the concept of propriety of compensation itself comes to be questioned. It is not simply a question of calculation (of the proper compensation) but a question of whether and under what circumstances it is 'proper' to transfer a resource from one activity to another. This leads to a question that is important from the point of view of governance. This also questions the claim of unquestioned dominance of a single, defined ethics in this Age of Empire. From the community's perspective, the answer to the question of whether land can at all be reduced to an exchange value (which is always homogeneous, so comparable with other use values) erasing its common use value, can only be sought through a mode of decision-making that allows direct participation of the community.

To appreciate the analytical scope of this twist to the concept of PCA let us go to a field far removed from land acquisition. At the time when a furious debate was raging regarding the various issues raised by the Uruguay round of negotiations of

GATT, the head of the department of mathematics of a leading US university (I have forgotten the name) made a very perceptive comment to the effect that if the proposed patent regime was implemented then the individual scientist would be richer but science would be poorer. In our scheme the reference is to the first alienation in the process of PCA. At this moment knowledge ceases to remain a common property and becomes private property. As common property the use value of knowledge is determined by the 'needs' of the community. These needs would include, apart from the requirement of solving the problems emanating from production, the intellectual pleasure of the pursuit of knowledge. Once knowledge becomes a private property it is simply exchange value to the individual who develops it. It is use value to the one who buys it. But what is this use value? Presumably a firm will pay for the patent rights to this knowledge. The firm invests in this acquisition only because it speculates that this is a profitable venture. So use value and exchange value become strangely inseparable, vindicating an inaugural insight of Spivak. Before the enforcement of patent rights knowledge communication and development were linked to, among other things, the common human urge to 'know'. The easy dissemination of knowledge is a condition for the fulfilment of this urge in society at large. At the same time common participation in the development of knowledge would itself restrain the development of knowledge along lines that are harmful to humanity. At the next stage of PCA, which the professor did not elaborate, the wherewithal to develop this private property—knowledge—would be concentrated in the hands of capital. At this moment the individual scientist would be a paid employee, with no rights to his/her inventions.

Before we go on to outline what could be the elements of a counter hegemonic strategy in this context let us try to deal with an of the obvious fallacy of our analysis. Knowledge pursuit that is not ordered by the rules of private property could be differently constrained but could similarly constrict the knowledge horizons of society. This is what the history of science in the West teaches us. We are not talking of such a common property rights to knowledge. So the community that we are talking of is itself an object of struggle, an ideal. Then are we not violating the tenets of the position from which we gained our initial theoretical insight—postmodernism? We plead guilty. Postmodernism can provide the tools for debunking a theory but it cannot provide a basis for counter hegemonic practice. To this manner of argumentation there is no hierarchy. Difference and mutual constitutivity is all. So we have to move out of its constraints—vulgarise it so to say. So the kind of commonality that lies at the base of our concept of common property in knowledge is one without hierarchy and so without power discrimination. This leads directly to the question of counter hegemonic strategy. The development of knowledge and the construction of this knowledge community must proceed simultaneously. Counter hegemonic practice will consist of this simultaneous struggle. It could consist of subversive strategies, but more importantly it will consist of the development of new technologies, of rules of knowledge dissemination that further community rights in knowledge. There are already attempts by concerned seekers to form communities where knowledge and information can be exchanged without the mediation of commodities. We can similarly imagine other communities that will circumvent the commodity nexus in say the field of games, art, etc. These communities will not initially be interlinked. One could be part of a knowledge community and at the same time belong to the capital-commodity order that runs the spectacle called games.

Fundamentally in all spheres one must try to revitalise the community content of use value at the cost of the subjective, individual use values. There must be a simultaneous effort to construct a community within which this sense can be nurtured. There are various examples of efforts in this direction. The on going experiments with the *Shramajibi haspataal*s are a step in this direction. These efforts have a lot in common with the attempts of many rural communitarians like Tagore in the pre-independence period. The essence of Tagore's teachings in this regard was that the most pernicious effect of the coming of the British was that the population became dependent on the benevolence of the state like never before. Before the British invasion the Indian rural community was unique in its autonomy from central authority. They managed their productive, social and legal problems on their own. The British changed all that and made the people on the state to tackle their every problem. So the principal requirement for the rejuvenation of the country was to begin its economic revival without the assistance of the state. For this a dedicated cooperative movement (*Samabay)* had to be built and sustained.

The attitude to the state, what could be the principles of law and property appropriate to such orders, all these and many related questions will have to be solved in the course of the movement to revive or create these cooperatives. There will of course be unavoidable clashes with state power. But the difference with what is taught as an axiom by Marxist parties that have not been subjugated by the ruling commodity culture is clear. The movement must not be organised with the sole objective of capturing state power—rather the objective must be one of construction of state power from the grass root, struggle to construct alternate modes of common property and their utilisation.

Signing Off

These are very tentative suggestions so the question of reaching a conclusion does not arise. The principle objective of this piece was to search for the theoretical building blocks that can be used for construction of a counter hegemonic strategy. I believe that unless we can clarify our theoretical perspectives movements like those that are resisting the government's efforts to grab land are likely to be misappropriated. And I am not talking of conscious subversive take over—that is a simple fact that can be effectively handled. I am talking of an unconscious derailment of such movements faced with the absence of a destination.

May 25, 2007

References

Basu, 2007. Basu, P.K.,*Political Economy of Land Grab, Economic and Political Weekly,* April 7-13, 2007.

Dobb, 1973. Dobb, M., *Theories of Value and Distribution Since Adam Smith*, Cambridge University Press, Cambridge, 1973.

Marx, 1954. *Capital*, Vol. I, Progress Publishers, Moscow, 1954. reprint, 1974.

Negri and Hardt, 2000. Negri, A. and Hardt, M., *Empire*. Harvard University Press, Cambridge, 2000.

Spivak, 1987. Spivak, G., *Speculations on Reading Marx After Reading Derrida* in *Post Structuralism and the Question of History*. Ed. Attridge, Derrick, et al. Cambridge University Press, Cambridge, 1987.

5

The Return of the Repressed: Explanation of the Left Front Defeat in West Bengal

Anjan Chakrabarti

The scale of defeat of the Left Front in West Bengal can hardly be underestimated. We are not merely talking about quantity here; this after all is its first election defeat in 32 years. The Left Front's aura of invincibility and the authority that flows from it has collapsed. For me this election is historic for producing this momentous break in the psychic relation between the people and the Left Front. The Law of the Father is gone and so are the respect, fear and anxiety that went with it; the mass, including even the opposition, is taking time to come to terms with this realisation. Whether the Left Front can recover or not from this debacle is a long-term question, but no matter what happens, from now on, its existence and electoral fortunes will be vulnerable in the same way as those of the other parties.

Explanation of the CPI(M) for the Defeat

Once upon a time, by virtue of being associated with a Communist Party, I met many communists with courage, courage to accept things (no matter how uncomfortable) as they are, rather than live in denial. I realise nowadays this is no easy human attribute and nowhere do I find this better demonstrated than in the current leadership of the Left Front in West Bengal.

Biman Bose, the state general secretary, has said this defeat reflects a UPA 'wave' and that it has nothing to do with the West Bengal situation. If the Left had stayed with the UPA by ignoring the nuclear deal, then the alliance of the Congress with TMC would not have materialised and this defeat could have been avoided. Nirupam Sen, the chief architect of the capitalist development model in West Bengal, has argued that this result has nothing to do with local issues; it is instead an endorsement of the UPA. Let me spend some time with this hypothesis.

First, the 'wave' thing. Such is the scale of the psychic disconnection between the people and this leadership that it seems to have confused the meaning of a wave; and coming as it does from a senior communist, politburo member and a state general this is tragic and comical at the same time. We saw a wave once after the death of Indira Gandhi; while the consequent scale of Rajiv Gandhi's victory is well known it needs reminding that even then the Left Front bucked the trend and emerged victorious in West Bengal. Moreover, the UPA has not even secured a simple majority; to call this a wave is indeed a very 'thoughtful' explanation. Finally, a cursory look at the surrounding states of West Bengal reveals the UPA lost heavily in Jharkhand, Bihar and Orissa. This 'wave'-based explanation is a reflection of a culture of denial that has gripped the leadership of the party and has percolated down to the lowest rung in the party hierarchy. Evidently, it will only help reiterate and reinforce the psychic dissonance I referred to earlier. And there is an underlying tragedy here that says a lot about the current state of the CPI(M). It is this: it is not that these 'communists' do not know; the tragedy is that 'they do not know that they do not know'. They do not even know that a psychic dissonance has appeared. Rabindranath Tagore called this human state of *avidya* or ignorance troubling and painful while Jonathan Lear called it comical. I leave it to the readers to make a pick of what it is.

Second, this hypothesis may have a loop of its own, which has the following effect: it helps everybody to avoid taking responsibilities. Nobody needs to take blame and everybody is happy. My point is simple: the culture of critical self-reflection has virtually disappeared from the CPI(M). Instead, a sharp division between the inside and outside has appeared; the tendency is always to find an external entity to solve the problems (such as through the state) and to put the blame on (such as the US, intellectuals, media, Karat, etc.). Some part of the latter may be true but the point is that such a blame game has its contradictory effect. The light never turns on oneself; it is always turning to the others; the Self remains, literally, in a shadow of darkness. The CPI(M) in West Bengal, as it stands now, has cast itself in the armour of darkness; that there is a psychic dissonance between it and the people should come as no surprise.

My Explanation of the Left Front Defeat

All evidences direct us to the fact that the election was fought in West Bengal fundamentally on a local plank: on the TMC side the issue was *Ma* (capturing the issue of women's predicament in Left Front rule), *Mati* (the land question capturing the right of people principally peasants over land) and *Manush* (the human rights question that is said to have been violated repeatedly under the Left Front) and on the side of the CPI(M) it was capitalist-sponsored industrial development. The verdict is resoundingly clear: the former has triumphed over the latter. That is not to say the central leadership's position on the nuclear deal leading to the withdrawal of support to the government and its effort of putting together an unconvincing third front was not a contributing factor, but it was only a contributing factor to the 'wave of discontent' that has already started forming in West Bengal over the past few years. It is to the credit of Mamata Banerjee (credit has to be given where it is due) that she harnessed the discontents from multiple sides into a tidal wave of opposition that swept away the Left Front. The questions are: why did *Ma*, *Mati* and *Manush* win over capitalist-induced industrial development? More particularly, what happened in the intermittent period of the sweeping victory of the Left Front in the 2006 West Bengal assembly polls and its collapse in vote bank in 2009? Some major local factors that seem to have worked are the following:

(i) ***Land Grab:*** The first factor is clearly Singur and Nandigram. The kind of cataclysmic collapse of Left Front vote (its vote percentage dropping by an astonishing 8 per cent) can only be explained by an eruption of some magnitude that altered the symbolic meaning attached to the CPI(M) in a fundamental way, from its positive connotation to a negative one. Despite accusations of rights violation, abuse of power, nepotism, and so on, the people of West Bengal deposited faith in the Left Front for over 30 years because they connected with it on one axis: it was considered the gatekeeper of the poor and marginalised. The effect of Singur and Nandigram was this: the symbolic relation of the Left Front to the poor disappeared in one shot. The CPI(M)'s authority that flowed from this symbolic relation was not just physical but also an ethical one. With the collapse of this ethical authority, its physical authority took on a different proportion in the minds of the people. The physical authority—reflected not only in the working of the government but also that of the local committees—became a matter of bullying and sheer violence rather than necessary or defensive; for the right or wrong reasons, the violence from the TMC side started appearing as defensive and necessary. The sight of the CPI(M) working in tandem with the police to evict farmers from land, shooting its constituents (including women) and abusing its citizens, and that too for a bunch of abrasive capitalists, helped snap the psychic relation of the people with the Left Front. It was as if a case of the father turning his gun on his mother and children (it is after all a self-proclaimed party of the peasants and workers); it constituted in the eyes of many an *adharma* of monumental proportions. For many who had traditionally supported the Left, especially in the rural heartland, it turned the relation with the CPI(M) from one of respect and fear to that of anxiety and hatred; *Mati* started appearing as a societal question; the movement for land and against the government-sponsored policy of land grab-based industrial development soon acquired a momentum of its own across Bengal. The strong defence of the Left Front government for capitalist industrialisation that often took a rhetorical turn against agriculture per se further alienated the agrarian populace who saw this relentless campaign of slight towards agrarian forms of life as further proof of the Left Front's pro-rich shift.

(ii) ***Working Class Shift:*** It was expected by the CPI(M) that the development model of capitalist industrialisation would gain the support of the workers and urbanites. It did not happen. The workers, who had traditionally supported the Left, moved in droves to vote against the Left Front. Multiple factors contributed to this. First, the rhetoric of new jobs via industrialisation sounded hollow in many industrial areas, especially on both sides of the Ganges, where factories have been closing down leaving tens of thousands unemployed. Second, in many places, the Left Front trade unions came to be seen as cronies of capitalists and working against the interest of the workers; in some cases, they were even seen as contributing to the closure of the factories. Third, the government's effort to push through the industrialisation effort called for a peaceful trade union. With the workers already under attack from the capitalists, this passive role of Left Front trade unions was increasingly seen suspiciously by the workers. All such factors and perhaps many more moved the workers to push the voting button in favour of the TMC.

Moreover, while it could very well be the case that some rich urbanites may have responded positively to the industrialisation campaign, the fact remains that it did not cut much ice with the middle-income group and in all respects backfired with the urban poor who increasingly came to identify the CPI(M) as pro-rich.

(iii) ***Shift of Intellectuals:*** The sight of land acquisition and abuse of people (especially women) had a tremendous negative effect on the intellectuals of Bengal, who traditionally were on the side of the Left. They not only went en masse against the Left Front but also joined the movement of *Ma, Mati* and *Manush* that Mamata Banerjee had now made her agenda to fashion a return to her low political fortune; it is my belief that the Left Front grossly underestimated the effect of this campaign by the intellectuals on the people, urban and rural; cultural interventions, and that too with political messages, after all do shape minds.

(iv) ***Minority Trouble:*** One must talk about the 'Muslim' factor, which it seems has shifted decisively towards Mamata Banerjee. The fact that many of the affected peasants in Singur, Nandigram and elsewhere were Muslims had a profound effect on that community. Moreover, the Rizwanur Rahman case and the Sachar committee report on the minorities were major contributing factors in the shaping of this community's vote, which has till now been steadfastly with the Left Front, against the CPI(M).

(v) ***Incompetent Governance:*** After Singur and Nandigram, the Left Front government came to be increasingly seen as incapable to govern. In the eyes of many, this was a case of weak and incompetent government with such a strong majority. Moreover, it was seen as acting in a biased manner. It was seen as siding with the CPI(M), the rich, capitalists and promoters, and unable to maintain law and order. Eruption of various other movements such as in Lalgarh over police atrocities, in Kolkata over the Rizwanur Rahman case as also by the autoworkers and hawkers, in various districts over the failure of the public distribution system and the sustained statehood movement in Darjeeling reinforced the belief that this government is inept; in all these cases, the state was seen as backtracking, vacillating and surrendering.

Finally, charges of utter failure in the sectors of education, health and elementary infrastructure (roads, drinking water, etc.) at the village and town level found resonance with the people. A debate has started to emerge in West Bengal as to the overall meaning of development: should it be reduced to capitalist-sponsored industrial development or should its meaning be seen in a wider extension where industry is one among many nodes of progress. Mamata Banerjee's TMC has started to craft a meaning of development along the second line and that is what they campaigned for. In doing so, they could criticise on one hand what they claimed to be the failure of the Left Front to provide the mass with basic development amenities and the other hand fend off charges of being anti-developmentalist. Turning away from the industry-versus-agriculture debate, Mamata had taken the position of the coexistence of industry and agriculture: in her words, they are brother and sister existing side by side. Against this, the CPI(M)'s position hit the public as a proposal for industrial development through a breakdown of agriculture; evidently, it was more dramatic but one that alarmed the rural populace in ways yet to be fully comprehended.

(vi) ***When Love became Repression:*** The control over social life that the CPI(M) party exercised through its local committees appeared, for a large segment of the population, increasingly as a control over their life by an external entity; it simply became intolerable over time. Local issues, sometimes even family issues, at the ground level in which the local committees would invariably intervene with its unrecorded punitive justice system began to be seen as undue encroachment; their proclaimed 'help' became in the eyes of many as the 'power of the muscle'. More and more, its machinery came to seen as an instrument of abuse that function on modalities of threats, punishment, prohibition and segregation of whoever was considered an opponent; a system of 'witch-hunting' had enveloped the party structure in the way it dealt with the people; 'either you are with me' or else.... It came to be seen more and more as procreating a culture of moral policing. Its technology of control that was once celebrated as efficient machinery by the pundits has now become a liability. For many, the feeling of repression enacted through the daily control with its cloud of the 'power of the muscle' found their determined release in the form of Mamata Bannerjee, who presented herself as the new messiah of the poor and the abused; her strident anti-CPI(M) stand was enough reason for many to vote for the TMC. The stage was set for the vanguards (the party of educators) to be taught a lesson and vanquished.

(vii) ***The Rise of the Sahaj:*** This argument may not appear direct or could even be seen as tangential, but I think it points to a fundamental shift in the body politic of West Bengal. The Left Front's industrial development model is supposed to usher in change in the future, which though demanded sacrifice in the present. The problem is that often the burden of this sacrifice falls unequally on the 'poor' and at least the current generation cannot see what would happen in the future; as for that matter, nobody knows what would happen in the future. For the poor, this is too much of a risk. Not only that. There is more.

For me, Singur and Nandigram was a great learning point. I have since wondered: why did the peasants say no to development? When peasants could be heard as saying that he would not give up his land for all the wealth of the world, I realised that this flowed from a totally different worldview, something that cannot be fathomed either in the mainstream economics or the historical materialist approach. I have seen many friends jump into a conclusive description of Singur and Nandigram as a case of primitive accumulation. I have no issue with them; these were indeed that; they also correctly pointed out that Marx did not describe let alone defend primitive accumulation; he critiqued primitive accumulation. But I wondered about something else which I thought is a deeper issue, something that would perhaps go on to capture the uniqueness of the unfolding primitive accumulation in India. It came with this realisation that the subjects here, at least in Bengal, are espousing a totally different worldview as compared to that on which the policies of the Left Front government were being based upon: there was serious disconnect between the language of the policymakers/party apparatchik and that of the people. In the former, not only was time considered as split (past and future), but the reality seen as fragmented and segmented. In this somewhat modernist/westernised worldview, it was easy to see the land, water, forest, and so on as the objects that are detached from the subject. This objectified worldview made it possible to administer over 'things,' perform cost-benefit and decide on the price of giving up land (compensation, resettlement and so on).

But, what if subjects do not see the world in this way; what if their forms of life conform to a worldview that is fundamentally different. What if they see the world as espoused by Tagore (he called this the philosophy of the Indian way of life, the life of *sahaj* or simple):

> ...the mere process of addition did not create fulfilment; that mere size of acquisition did not produce happiness; that greater velocity of movement did not necessarily constitute progress, and that

> change could only have meaning in relation to some clear ideal of completeness.

Pardon me for being somewhat forceful, but this is no mere philosophical speculation, but something that had been imbibed in the Indian way of life since the inception of its civilisation. Water, land and forest, to name some, are not external objects as perhaps in a westernised outlook, but are seen in unity with the self; this is part of the experience of the *sahaj*. To use Tagore again, the man with a 'scientific' outlook

> ...will never understand what it is that the man with the spiritual vision finds in these natural phenomena. The water does not merely cleanse his limbs, but it purifies his heart; for it touches his soul. The earth does not merely hold his body, but it gladdens his mind; for its contact is more than a physical contact – it is a living presence. When a man does not realise his kinship with the world, he lives in a prison-house whose walls are alien to him.... In India men are enjoined to be fully awake to the fact that they are in the closest relations to things around them, body and soul, and that they are to hail the morning sun, the flowing water, the fruitful earth, as the manifestation of the same living truth which holds them in its embrace.

This is not a wisdom that is simply applicable to rural areas, but also urban areas, especially the urban poor and the lower-middle income group. One can neither ignore the dissonance in the cultural understanding of time. The meaning of time in industrial development is artificial and limited (past and future); we know where it came from: Western Europe. This, on the other hand, is a land which resonates with the following theses of the Baul singers:

> I would not go, my heart, to Mecca or Medina, For behold, I ever abide by the side of my Friend. Mad would I become, had I dwelt afar, not knowing Him. There is no worship in Mosque or Temple or special holy day. At every step I have my Mecca and Kashi; sacred is every moment.

The concept of time here is that of the *sahaj* where it is neither limited nor artificial but timeless, where culture does not conceive forms of life in terms of some future, but as something procreating in all times. In the worldview of the *sahaj*, space is not split into a temporal verticality (backward and forward) that introduces the idea, a quite artificial idea, of progress as a movement from the backward to the forward. Instead, life is seen as moving horizontally at each moment of time; life is to be lived and connected to at each moment; space, time and life is connected in relationality rather than seen as fragmented. Life is about rhythm, harmony and balance, and only in such completeness does life acquire any meaning where the theme of life is unity and not fragmentation. It is not that no kind of segmentation exists in such societies, but this sense of unity is also present, and strongly presently, side by side. Far from being uniform, the social space, at least in West Bengal, is a battle ground for two different and tension-ridden worldviews; what though, at the minimum, cannot be ignored is that the worldview of the *sahaj* is also a living presence.

What I am trying to say is that the worldview in terms of which the idea of capitalist-induced industrial development was conceived came to be seen as a total disconnect from the worldview of the *sahaj*. On the issue of land (and things like resettlement, compensation, etc.) the Left Front was talking in language of the former, which was not only alien to the latter but also threatening and humiliating. In the language of the 'Left Front'/modernist, the world of the *sahaj* was projected repeatedly as traditional, devalued and worthless; their labour is no labour, only industrial high-tech labour is labour; their experience of time, space and connection was rendered meaningless in this outlook. A party that once stood and fought for the *sahaj* appeared more and more foreign in its language, exposition and practice. The appearance and later (after Singur and Nandigram) specter of primitive accumulation translated as a form of resistance not just into a defence of the land, but also a way of life in its entirety. It is not that monetary compensation or resettlement was not to be discussed in any situation (one can very well imagine people wanting to shift their forms of life), but such relocations would now have to be accounted for in a different register..a political one. It was not longer to be a case of top down approach of the policy makers and bureaucracy who tell the peasants (and hawkers, autoworkers and so on) what should happen, but is now more a face to face encounter with the affected. The 'terms' of dealing and negotiation has fundamentally changed in the last two years in West Bengal; it is the reiteration again of the supremacy of the 'poor' over the body politic.

In contrast, Mamata connected directly with the rhythm of this language; she spoke not only in the language of the *sahaj*, but also defended that experience. For the elite in the cities steeped in modernist thinking, Mamata often appears as 'irrational,' some call her as symbolising 'unreason' reflecting the fact that they cannot understand her language and her concerns, that she tends to go against what are seen as 'normal' facets of modern life. Her 'irrationality' or her 'unreason' is a broader issue for me reflecting the total disconnect of modernist India (within which the CPI(M) is now embedded) from the experience of the *sahaj*. The relation of the politics to language relates to the exposition of politics, and that becomes a decisive factor at times as it did in this case. Politics is simply not about facts, measurement and voting games; when it takes the shape of the return of the 'unreason' it becomes a different ball game. As I understand, this election captured such a shift in West Bengal. It is not merely a defeat of the Left Front, but a defeat that has seriously dented the hegemony of the modernist worldview; in its immediate future, whoever comes to power now in West Bengal would find himself confronted by a strong and living presence of the *sahaj* that will find its release in the power of the 'poor'. The battle line between the TMC and the CPI(M) has given way to a parallel battle between the 'poor'.

Leftism and Mamata

It is at times astonishingly for me to imagine how the party leadership could miss the possible psychic effect of the *adharma* of Singur and Nandigram in their political imagination. But then this is the point: perhaps they do not even know this is *adharma*. This *avidya*—which shows off in arrogance and disdain—made the psychic dissonance grow deeper; the disbelief that a Left Front government could shoot its constituency—the peasants—started acquiring the momentum of anger; this anger was in no way circumscribed within the boundary of the peasants. If the US bombing in distant Vietnam could cause tumult in the minds of the Bengali people, to imagine that something of this proportion happening so close to home would not have any effect is truly astonishing; to think of Singur and Nandigram as a local issue as some CPI(M) leaders suggested points to the kind of bankruptcy in thought that had set in the party. Actually, this also points to a different problem for the Left generally: they are so much enmeshed in a structuralist way of looking at the world that they cannot fathom the role played by subjectivity formation in politics. Anyway, it is important to realise that, in its multiple dimensional effects, Singur and Nandigram transformed the psychic relation of the people with the CPI(M), something that not only affected the poor but also the other segments of the population that had supported the Left Front. It reinforced those who were opposed to the Left (thereby closing any possibility of their being won over) and alienated many steadfast supporters of the Left. In fact, a large segment of the Left intellectuals have critiqued, through newspapers, little magazines, TV, CDs and even books, the Left Front as the new right which I believe had an enormous effect on many traditional Left supporters. Additionally, what was made easier for the latter to make the shift was the complete makeover of Mamata Banerjee and her self-proclaimed image now as more of a Leftist than the Left Front. This is the final point I want to make.

I have a thesis: no party can win elections in West Bengal if it is not seen as Leftist in orientation. This explains the peculiarity of West Bengal as compared to the rest of the country. First through social reforms and then through long decades of movements in which the Left itself played an instrumental role, the 'poor' has come to acquire a voice, an assertive political voice. It is though not just that. What has also come to fruition is the alignment of a certain segment of the middle class with the mindset that the voice of the 'poor' (this is a catchall term standing for small farmers, industrial and agrarian workers and other 'marginalised' groups)will be the final arbiter in any dispute. For right or wrong reasons, the Left Front had come to occupy this moral authority of being the party of the 'poor' (its own movements earlier were responsible for its rise) and its uninterrupted rule was firmed up by this belief among a section of the populace. Mamata Banerjee, whose one-point programme had long been singularly an anti CPI(M) position, tried various permutations and combinations to dislodge the Left Front, flirting with both the BJP and the Congress. She failed every time. She failed because the mentioned symbolic authority of the Left Front remained intact. It is to her credit that Mamata realised this, and in this she was probably helped by many previously Naxalite leaders who joined her since the Singur and Nandigram movement. Step by step, as part of a carefully chalked out strategy (those who think of Mamata as just eccentric are simply living in a fools' paradise), Mamata hammered at the symbols that defined the psychic relation of the people with the Left Front. She even called herself the rightful heir of the Tebhaga movement and the Food movement that were some of the symbols, which helped establish the pro-poor symbolic attachment of the people with the CPI(M) and the Left Front. Separating Marx and Leftism from the Left Front, she turned her criticism of the CPI(M) into the following: the Left Front and the CPI(M) have forsaken the traditional constituencies of the Left and they have no relation with Leftism. It is she who now is a Leftist fighting for the cause of the poor and marginalised against the Left Front, which wants to usher in industrial development for the capitalists at their expense. If politics is also about symbols as I do believe it is, Mamata turned the hitherto accepted division between Left and Right upside down thereby making it easier for many traditional Left thinkers, activists and voters to cross over to her camp. She has virtually usurped the issues which were previously considered as the domain of the Left Front and left the Left Front fighting the elections on one plank: industrial development to be sponsored by capitalists. The contrast and the turn of the table in the contrast could not be any starker in the position taken with respect to the SEZ debate where Mamata turned totally against the idea of SEZ while the CPI(M) supported it. Take another example. The elections saw Mamata start her campaign from Nandigram and she took its soil to her election meetings: a powerful symbolic connection that related to the hearts of the people. In contrast, to the astonishment of many, the CPI(M)'s campaign revolved around the symbol of 'Nano' that not only captured the strange relation of communists with capitalists but also appealed to the minds and not the hearts of people. Where *Mati* is not just an economic component (as in the West) but an integral segment of people's forms of life, in the land of social movements, revolutionaries and poets, this battle between the soul and the material was no contest.

Mamata presented herself as the champion of the poor, of peasants and workers and anybody who claimed themselves as vulnerable and hard done by the government policies or the CPI(M). In the eyes of many, she has emerged as the Leftist par excellence and the Left Front as keeper of capitalists, promoters and power brokers. It was after having made this image makeover that Mamata opted for an alliance with the Congress; qualitatively, the meaning of this alliance took on a different dimension than previous such unsuccessful alliances, an aspect that the CPI(M) did not quite understand. Due to this qualitative alteration, it is my firm belief that had there being no alliance the results still would not have changed fundamentally.

I do not know whether the Left Front and the CPI(M) will reflect on the clear psychic dissonance that has appeared between it and the people. But to do that they have to be awake first and to be awake they have to accept the reality: the act of *adharma* in various axes. Mistakes can be made and even sins are committed. But our sages have taught that the Lights shine on those who accept the responsibility for their actions; the sin is washed away, the shame turned into an act of courage. But on those who do not even recognise their sins and mistakes, it is said that a pall of darkness awaits their future; there is no stopping their downfall and ultimately demise. What I find alarming is a complete ignorance of this wisdom on the part of the Left Front as of now.

Some Reflections for Marxists in India

I believe that this election result is a watershed in the history of the Leftist movement in India. It has shown a few things: (i) no self-proclaimed Marxist party can forward a path of capitalist development and get away with it in a democratic set up like India, (ii) there is a serious need to rethink the idea of vanguardism in a scenario where repressive apparatuses are coupled with strong and deep ideological apparatuses and (iii) state-oriented and not movement-oriented politics has severe limitation for Marxian parties. The tragedy is, and this I have and am resolutely ready to defend, these do not have any necessary connection with Marx. Regarding the first point, it is my contention that Marx did not describe let alone defend primitive accumulation (as the West Bengal CPI(M) leadership was apparently doing in order to defend its policy of land grab in bringing about capitalism as a necessary moment of historical evolution of society); instead, Marx critiqued primitive accumulation; that was the purpose of producing that concept in the first place; Marx was no historicist, but rather a critique of the 'science' of history as the debate on Russian Road showed so clearly. Secondly, Lenin's vanguardism was construed by keeping the repressive apparatus in mind and hence is inadequate in this situation; it has its own series of problems and some of its showed in the kind of party bureaucracy that had become not all of which need be discussed here. One among these though I should point out: the organisational structure based on the division between party exclusivity and the rest of the population that is the defining moment of vanguardism is the source of many problems encountered later in the name of Marxism. It is neither necessary nor inevitable to think of organisation along the Leninist line. Lenin had the courage to ask: what is to be done? Can we show a similar courage at the dawn of the 21st century? Third, the state-dependent approach of the Left (whether through a parliamentary or extra parliamentary route) is a joke on Marx who based his entire political philosophy of freedom on an anti-state plank; otherwise, his search for commune makes no sense. Marx, who was looking for creative union, found the state as external to the people: how can communion be created with something that is 'external' to people and has been conceptualised to govern from top down? The point is not that the state is to be ignored; it cannot be ignored and that is not what I am suggesting here. Instead, the issue is whether the idea of politics will be state-dependent or focused on enacting social transformation; the difference will produce two different kinds of politics. One of the most remarkable phases of Marxism in the 20th century has been the occulting of Marx produced through the displacements of its idea of politics from initiating ground-level social change to a state-dependent, policy-oriented approach; the effect of this bureaucratisation of the idea of Left politics can hardly be underestimated as the Left Front experience has shown.

These western Marxian ideas adopted uncritically by the Indian communist movement had produced a sad situation: a country that provides fertile ground and potential for Left movement has seen stagnation and in fact a decline (in many parts) of the Left imagination. At least, those who are unshackled by the *avidya* shown by the Left Front till now can start this introspection at a serious level; it is not a matter of changing this here or there but of rethinking the entire milieu of what it means to be a Marxist in the Indian context. The question is: are there courageous Marxists available in the Left circle and that includes the Left Front?

May 21, 2009

6

India's Move to the Right

Pothik Ghosh

This is not a practical joke. Something really outrageous has happened. The overwhelming victory of the Congress-led United Progressive Alliance (UPA) in the 15th Lok Sabha elections has meant an unqualified triumph for the sangh parivar's ideological agenda. Of course, if one were to look for the emergence of an electoral centre consonant with such an ideological triumph—as the one symbolised by the Congress in the first two-and-a-half decades of Independence —one would find nothing to substantiate this. The BJP-led National Democratic Alliance (NDA) is, with regard to the UPA, the second-largest coalition by far. One cannot, therefore, be faulted for dismissing the above claim as a product of an exaggeratedly apocalyptic imagination that loves to poop a glorious party.

But such, alas, is the irony of the situation that the BJP no longer needs to emerge as the leader of Parliament to culminate the sangh's programme of establishing a majoritarian national political centre. And wasn't this the RSS's cherished dream after all, something that prevented it from seriously pursuing the project of backing a political party of its own for the first few decades of its inception? Well, that dream has come true when the Sangh Parivar least expected it, needless to say, despite the RSS and its political face.

No sense can, however, be discerned in this seemingly

quixotic explanation unless the victory of liberalism, which the Congress's thumping electoral win signifies, is located in its current historical moment. Otherwise, it would imply an uncritical acceptance of certain pre-given notions of liberalism. The Congress today, thanks to its current electoral revival as a strong centre of Indian polity, is similar to its post-Independence predecessor only in appearance. The consensus that has driven its current re-emergence is significantly and qualitatively different from the one that underpinned its earlier Nehruvian-liberal edition, and which collapsed under the weight of its own contradictions through the 1960s and 70s to unfold into Indira Gandhi's Emergency and the Jayaprakash Narayan-led anti-Congress movement.

Development is the new shibboleth of the current Congress consensus and the liberal political centre it has purportedly propped up. And this new avatar of development has played, and will continue to play, a crucial role in shaping the social content of this consensus, even as it leaves its political idiom of liberal-secular citizenship intact. The aggressively competitive political-economic ethos of this neoliberal form of development—which is geared towards socio-economic restructuring through alienation of people from their assets that are their means of life and/or livelihood—has come to increasingly determine what this constitutionally-ordained idea of liberal-secular citizenship actually amounts to in the everyday lives of individuals.

This process of total commodification of hitherto non-commodified or semi-commodified sectors of society and economy through coercive politico-economic and legislative practices—which Marx termed primitive accumulation of capital and which American economic-geographer David Harvey has redefined for our late capitalist times as "accumulation by dispossession"—will continue to shape the inner socio-political contours of the ideology of liberalism with renewed political legitimacy. The secular idea of a culturally neutral citizenship will, in such circumstances, become even more contingent on who gains from, and therefore naturally backs, this kind of development.

It is, therefore, hardly surprising that competitive identity politics, which has always driven electoral competition in Indian society but which has never received overt sanction in its liberal-democratic polity, has of late been turning into a politically legitimate impulse of neoliberal development that thrives on and encourages competitive dispossession of some socio-political groups by others. For, how else does one explain myriad incidents of land acquisition, effected through legislative changes and other repressive means by various state and central governments that enjoy the support of certain configurations of socio-economic and cultural identities which gain from such development?

That, however, is not the only way in which competitive dispossession, which is the dominant spirit of the reigning neo-liberal orthodoxy, has played out in this country. More indirect and legislatively less 'legitimate' means, not directly attributable to governments and their developmental agenda, have also been in evidence. The impulse of certain sections of the Hindu middle class of Gujarat to loot and destroy Muslim businesses, with a little more than tacit support from the BJP-led state government, during the 2002 post-Godhra carnage can, for instance, be located in socio-political, economic and cultural anxieties fostered by an intensely competitive ethos of a preponderantly expropriative political economy of neoliberal development.

Clearly, citizenship, and its entitlements, remain as culturally neutral and secular as before but the access to development that enables the acquisition of such liberal-secular credentials is paved, now more legitimately than ever, with the bloody bricks of socio-economic and cultural cleansing of some identities by others.

That even the struggles of those socio-cultural identities, which have been at the receiving end of such dehumanising development, have failed to transcend the logic of competition and expropriation intrinsic to this neoliberal developmental programme, proves there has been no political questioning of that model of development. Their struggles, whenever they have had the opportunity to move beyond defensive positioning, have ended up being contests where the subalterns have vied with the elite social groups to corner the privilege the latter enjoy. Those struggles, even as they have been directed at privileged and socially dominant groups and identities, have failed to focus on the neoliberal logic of development that such elite groups both embody and are a function of.

This failure of subaltern groups to transform the competitive nature of their challenge—which is how such challenges are bound to be posed to begin with—into a critique of the current political-economic system and its model of development has ended up shattering their initial anti-elite solidarity, evident right through the JP movement up to the Mandal period and the ascendancy of the V. P. Singh-led National Front government in 1989. That has led to the degeneration of their politics into a regressive battle of social domination among themselves. The ideological expression of such degeneration is, for instance, evident in recent popular cultural histories written by various Dalit and backward-caste intellectuals of Uttar Pradesh and Bihar in the service of their politics of assertion. Not only do those historical accounts— some of which have been collected by social historian Badri Narayan into a book called *Upekshit Samudayon ka Atm Itihas* (Self Histories of Marginalised Peoples)—not question the idea of structuring society around a strong centre, they seek to build such centres to assert their caste dignity through their supremacist historiographies. Worse, they do so by often enough adopting the traditional terms and idioms of the exclusivist and oppressive Brahminical social discourse.

The decline in politico-ideological independence or electoral fortunes of various lower-caste, minority and regional political forces—which also includes the CPI(M)-led Left Front —in this Lok Sabha election is merely a manifestation of this troubling competitive identity politics within the subaltern camp. That has led to the gravitation of some of those outfits, and the 'natural' support base of the others, towards either the Congress or the BJP. A strong bipolar tendency in Indian polity, which the decline of such third forces portends, is nothing but a disturbing sign of consolidation of the neoliberal consensus.

The current ascendancy of the Congress, given that it coincides with the emergence of such a strong bipolar political tendency, is especially disturbing. Both the real and imagined victims of neoliberal development under this new Congress-led dispensation would, in the absence of any strong current of independent subaltern politics, come to rely on the BJP to politically articulate their competitive quest for development. That, needless to say, would prompt the BJP to pose the idea of liberal-secular citizenship, and the question of access to expropriative neoliberal development that frames this idea, in consonance with the competitive aspirations of social groups it would seek to represent. That the ideology the BJP would deploy at the grassroots to electorally mobilise its potential support base for this battle for modern development and secular citizenship would be cultural nationalism is a no-brainer. In fact, the shift in the BJP's political-ideological tack, post-Babri, anticipated precisely this peculiar sort of rightward movement in Indian polity. Since the late 1990s the party stopped posing the Muslim as a dangerous alien to the Hindu community of this country, and has instead taken to mounting a zealous defence of a culturally deracinated but majoritarian national identity, and a form of modern development that produces it, from the depredations of groups that it emphasises has originated from within certain "backward" cultural identities (jihad-backing Muslims or Maoist-supporting Dalit Christians of Orissa). It has obfuscated the real causes of socio-economic dispossession and politico-cultural disenfranchisement that underpin such phenomena. That the BJP has forged the secular/pseudo-secular distinction, appropriating the first category for itself while ascribing the second to its opponents, shows there need exist no contradiction between liberal theories and revanchist political practices today.

The electoral pressures that such politics of the BJP would inevitably generate for the Congress and other non-BJP forces in a system of representative democracy, especially one tending towards bipolarity, cannot be overstated. That would, among other things, bolster the ongoing process of socio-ideological homogenisation of policymaking and lawmaking, even as normative, party-based differences are belaboured ad nauseum. The eerie similarity in legislative and policy rhetoric across the political spectrum—especially vis-à-vis questions of development, "jihadi" terror and Maoist insurgency—shows how the BJP-Sangh's ideological project, with more than a little facilitation from the global neoliberal programme and its local secular backers, has indeed been universalised.

In such a situation—where the current neoliberal form of development is constitutive of a majoritarian conception of modern political identity that gets projected as democratic—politics conducted in terms of the traditional secular-communal divide is, at best, useless and, at worst, perilously misleading.

What India would see more and more now is aggressively competitive identity politics at the grassroots, often culminating in civil violence, and the winners of such amoral competition rising up to be legitimately welcomed by a normatively liberal-secular political centre as 'authentic' and 'enterprising' citizens of the nation. This is, doubtless, the epoch when fascism and liberalism not only come to each other's rescue, as Gramsci had observed, in their respective moments of regulatory crises, but coexist in harmonious complementarity in the same temporal moment at the social and political levels respectively.

It is nobody's case that the Congress and the liberal Indian polity were innocent about the ways of identity politics in their post-Independence heyday. Identity management, through competitive and differential distribution of patronage at the societal grassroots by a liberal polity, was the hallmark of the Nehruvian Indian National Congress—which was supported by the Brahmin-Muslim-Harijan combine in UP and Bihar, and the Kshatriya-Harijan-Adivasi-Muslim coalition in Gujarat—till at least the advent of the Emergency. But all grassroots Congress leaders, who emerged in legislative and parliamentary politics by dint of their victory in such identity struggles and the concomitant management of such intra-party competition, were ultimately tamed and chastened by the liberal-secular ethos of the party and polity. In other words, the identity loyalty of a particular leader that had launched him from the grassroots to the national polity was perforce sacrificed by him/her at the altar of liberal-secularism—still organic to the relatively more democratic culture of a pre-Independence, anti-colonial

Congress—while participating in the business of policymaking and legislation. Clearly, competitive identity politics, and the differential distribution of patronage it entails, existed as the hypocritical and illegitimate unconscious of the Nehruvian Congress and its post-Independence polity. And it was precisely this contradic-tion—ineluctable in political liberalism, thanks to the political-economy of capitalism from which it emanates—that led to the collapse of the original Congress consensus.

Now, of course, it is a different story. The liberal ideas of culturally neutral citizenship and secularism are empty concepts into which any social content, no matter how illiberal, undemocratic or retrograde, can be poured and legitimised. Identity-based patronage politics, which had either been eyed with contempt or concealed shamefacedly by mainstream political parties, all of which practised it, is now getting sanctified as inclusion (obviously differential and unequal) by its blessed contact with the neoliberal dogma of competitive development. The competitiveness that is intrinsic to such politics is no longer an ugly and reactionary secret that liberal politics needs to hide in its messy social closets. Given that globally acceptable neoliberal development is driven by something similar, it is openly celebrated. Such competitiveness constitutes the developmental dynamic that shapes the internal configurations and contours of the liberal form. Unlike in the period of the Nehruvian Congress, caste- and community-based leaders, irrespective of their party affiliations, are not tamed by the liberal idea of secular citizenship. Instead, they fundamentally redefine that idea, with regard to policies and laws, in terms of the interests of the social groups they represent.

'Democratic' competition, in the absence of an impulse to socio-ideologically contest the status quo, ends up strengthening the system and its twin-logic of political domination and economic expropriation. That is particularly true in this neo-liberal epoch, which is determined by the operational primacy of finance capital. Before the onset of the neoliberal era, a subaltern struggle, even if it was waged in the register of competitive identity politics, still had some fighting chance to posit a critique of the political economy of capitalism. Such competition for a slice of the developmental pie, by virtue of being directed at the state, automatically targeted the real sector of the economy that this state regulated. And considering that the real sector can respond more effectively to the autonomous needs of a society the less determined it is by the exigencies of international finance capital, the chances that competitive identity politics of subaltern groups in pre-neoliberal times could democratise the socio-economic system by seeking to democratise the state and polity were much more than today.

Similar identity-based competitive struggles for a share in the neoliberal development have served to deepen systemic inequality and lack of democracy the more they have succeeded. That is because the real economy of India, ever since it started opening up to the world, has come to be increasingly subordinated to the speculative and profit-seeking demands of international finance capital. The intensified financialisation of the Indian economy this has resulted in has ensured the country's real sector responds, not what members of Indian society would democratically and autonomously aspire to and demand, but what would yield profits in sectors on which international finance capital has placed its heaviest bets. As a consequence, the entire world of demand-and-supply, and the socio-economic realm of work and leisure constituted by it, has become totally administered, sometimes through repressive force but mostly through ideological production of consent. Development happens to be the mantra of that operation. In such a scenario, any social or political movement that seeks a share of such development cannot deepen democracy, not even objectively. It can only keep consolidating the system and its intrinsically undemocratic and inegalitarian political economy.

The Left—including its CPI(M)-led parliamentary bloc, and its various semi- and extra-parliamentary groups—has completely failed to recognise this peculiar impact of neo-liberalism and financialisation on Indian polity. Not surprisingly, they have continued to press ahead with their time-worn paradigms of politics. Subjective intervention by various Left groups, when it occurs through their proactive engagement with the disaffections and aspirations of various dispossessed and disempowered socio-economic and cultural groups, can transform the competitive identitarian idiom of their struggles into a fundamental critique of the neoliberal model of development. Only that, when it happens, can possibly yield, a real counter-hegemonic politics of resistance and restore to the Indian Left its lost political relevance.

Of course, the rejection of the CPI(M)-led Left Front's authoritarianism by the electorates of Kerala, and particularly West Bengal, which brought its Lok Sabha tally down from 60 in 2004 to 24 this time around, must be hailed, especially since it has also failed to pose an alternative political-economic model of development to the current neoliberal one, which it has all but normatively accepted. Yet, what must not be lost sight of is the LF's political degeneration has been challenged and supplanted, not by tendencies from within the progressive tradition of working class politics, but by the Trinamool Congress-Congress coalition, which will be an integral part of the next Union government. In such circumstances, the electoral decimation of the CPI(M)-led Stalinist Left has only accelerated and strengthened Indian polity's right-ward move.

Such a working-class challenge to the CPI(M) and its front is still desperately awaited to wipe out whatever remains of this degenerate Left, so that revolutionary politics can once again reclaim the trust of the broader toiling masses and mobilise them for an anti-neoliberal, anti-capitalist battle. But for such a politics to emerge, genuine working-class forces, many of whom are still part of the LF constituents, need to be clear-sighted about what actually went wrong with the CPI(M)-led Left Front. The reactive anti-CPI(M) position, which many Left groups and individuals hold, would be of little help on that score.

We must, for starters, understand that the LF's attempt to aggregate various anti-Congress, anti-BJP forces in the run-up to the 15th Lok Sabha polls, contrary to what the neo-liberal spinmeisters of our mainstream media have been contending, was not opportunist per se. The challenge, no matter how transient, posed by some caste and regional parties against the two principal political protagonists in question is actually a reflection of the disaffection of social identities that have been rendered provisionally subaltern, vis-à-vis the more privileged social groups patronised by those two parties. Considering that those privileged groups represent socio-economic and cultural domination—which the neoliberal developmental agenda engendered by a political system hegemonised by the Congress and the BJP has created—any competitive challenge posed to them and their two parties by the provisional subalterns and their outfits is, to begin with, also an immanent and implicit critique of the hegemony of the entire system, and the competitive and expropriative political-economic logic of development that constitutes it. Such implicit critique posits the possibility of producing a rupture in the given neoliberal conjuncture and thereby effect a complete social transformation.

However, if the immanence of this critique is not recognised and it is not consciously expressed by the movements that pose them, it ceases being the first unavoidable step towards counter-hegemonic politics, and ends up consolidating the hegemonic logic of competition, domination and monopolistic centre-building. The LF's failure to engage with such implicit critiques so that they can be taken to their logical anti-systemic denouement, has always been responsible for delivering one or the other of these anti-Congress, anti-BJP outfits to either the Congress-led UPA or the BJP-led NDA as a client or junior partner, depending upon the pragmatic calculus of immediate interests and benefits such forces embody. It is this failure of the LF that has always rendered all its attempts to forge an anti-Congress, anti-BJP front opportunistic. And the failure stems from the LF's fatally inverted mode of politics. Its tactics of sewing up such a third front would be electorally brilliant only if it was preceded by serious struggles that engaged with the disaffection of the subaltern support bases of anti-Congress, anti-BJP political forces and enabled them to articulate them in an anti-systemic and critical idiom of social and political transformation. Such an engagement would, as a matter of fact, make such front-building politically redundant for the CPI(M)-led Left Front's political advance.

The LF, however, seems obsessed with the absurd idea of driving social change through electoral politics and alliance-building for votes. And that, very clearly, is a symptom of its social-democratic malaise, which it contracted nearly three decades ago when it decided to give up the strong immunity of working-class struggles. It is this social-democratic degeneration that has prevented the LF to envision development as something that needs to fundamentally transform society and its constitutive political-economic logic by re-imagining the hierarchical and alienating configurations of power that are both envisaged and embodied by the modern state in all its different forms, including the liberal-democratic.

The LF's social-democratic cretinism—constitutive of the process of institutionalisation of the various working-class movements from which it emerged—is manifest not only in the growing authoritarianism with which its constituent parties and state governments are run, but also in its excessive reliance on a broad-based system of dispensing patronage to keep those governments going. Such wide, cadre-based distribution of political patronage is an inevitable regression of the social-democratic imagination. One that envisages social progress and the well-being of the working people and the poor essentially as a question of distributive justice, which it believes is achievable by merely regulating equitable distribution of a given basket of socio-economic entitlements. In such a 'Leftist' scheme there is no place for interventionist and transformative politics because the state, which is the instrument of such efficient regulation and equitable redistribution, is treated as a passive and neutral entity that only needs to be controlled.

The upholders of such social-democratic Leftism make no attempt, as a consequence, to rethink and transform the structure of the modern state through a process of constant critique and struggle directed against the political economy that makes such an alienated and coercive institution of power possible. From there to neo-liberalism it is, as we have seen, merely one small step. And what use can working-class politics possibly have for such 'Leftists' or their 'Leftism'?

May 21, 2009

7

The UPA Moment: Shadows of a Growing Crisis for the Indian State

Shankar Gopalakrishnan

Amid political fractures, a global economic crisis and rising social tensions, this term of the United Progressive Alliance government is coming to an end. To many, there has been little to distinguish this period in Indian history, and indeed if anything it is marked by a lack of change. Yet the UPA period has been one of tensions and contradictions, a period that threw up in sharp relief some of the developing tendencies of the Indian polity. In the few days left before we deal with the results of the elections, it may be time to consider these tendencies. The hypothesis that emerges is both hopeful and disturbing: India's ruling class appears to be heading towards an intensifying hegemonic crisis.

What does one mean by this? Hegemony, in Gramsci's sense of the term, is the maintenance of ruling class power through a combination of coercion with the consent of the oppressed, won by a "concrete coordination" of the material interests of the ruling class bloc with other social sections. At its most basic, a hegemonic crisis is thus a crisis of legitimacy. But it is also more than that. Hegemony is not a one way flow between rulers and ruled, a deceit perpetrated by the one upon the other. If we accept the proposition that the capitalist state is a *social relation*, one function of which is to *organise* the ruling bloc of class fractions (Poulantzas 1978), hegemony provides the ideological facet of this relationship, serving to discursively define social power. While legitimating the power of the ruling bloc of class fractions, the hegemonic ideology also inherently defines for that ruling bloc who its legitimate members are, and provides an "explanation" for how it achieved that power. Second, by defining the parameters of thinking about society, it shapes the perspective and limits within which both the oppressed and the ruling class fractions approach the polity. What this means is that a hegemonic crisis produces not only a crisis of legitimacy; it also produces an increasing incoherence of the ruling bloc and its fractions, as the ideological frame that identified their common socio-political interests ceases to "work." The net result is a *disarticulation* of social power, as both the legitimacy and the coherence of the dominant bloc deteriorate. My argument here is that we are witnessing a shift in this direction in India today, and the resulting conjuncture presents both dangers and possibilities for left and democratic forces.

The 2004 Elections

An analytical starting point for such an approach is the 2004 elections that brought the UPA to power. The 'shock' defeat of the NDA were both less and more significant than they were often believed to be at the time. It was less significant than it was made out to be by those who saw these elections as a decisive rejection of the NDA. The received "common sense" about this election, weaker now in light of the UPA's pronounced neoliberal inclinations, was that this was a vote against "reforms" and, to a lesser extent, Hindutva. Indeed, for several months afterwards, the English media saw repeated and increasingly ludicrous attempts to defend neoliberal reforms against this perceived setback ("a revolution of rising expectations", "it's all anti-incumbency", etc.).

Yet in fact the 2004 election results were by no means a 'wave' against the NDA. Though widespread and deep-rooted discontent existed, there was no political formation in the elections that focused such discontent beyond the regional and the issue-specific. The confusing result is best summarised by

Yogendra Yadav: "The case that this was a mandate against policies of economic reforms is an overstatement... having said this, it is equally necessary to realise that... if this election could [have been] a referendum on economic reforms, the policies of liberalisation would have been rejected" (Yadav 2004). Nor was there any sense of an overwhelming defeat for the social bloc that had supported the NDA, a combination of upper castes and upper classes (Yadav 1999).

This reality, and the intensity with which the UPA has embraced neoliberalism, has led many on the left to argue that there was no significant difference between the two periods. But it is here that we underestimate the importance of 2004. For the consequence of an electoral result need not only be in direct shifts of political power; it can also operate at the discursive, ideological and political levels. In this sense, the elections of that year did indeed have a significant impact.

For a decisive defeat was indeed suffered in that year— not by the ruling coalition, but by the ruling class intelligentsia, and in particular by the key ideological forum of the "new India": the English media. The defensiveness of neoliberals in the English media was not merely an overreaction. This intelligentsia had steadfastly predicted the return of the NDA and, in a symbiotic partnership with the bureaucracy and the party leadership, crafted the understanding whose preeminent symbol was "India Shining." 2004 not only showed that this ideology had failed to secure hegemonic or even dominant status in Indian politics; it also demonstrated a more fundamental failure. Indeed, 2004 was both a *transition* for elements of the ruling bloc and a *symptom* of a deeper failure.

Hegemony and the Indian Neoliberal Project

In itself the media's behaviour may seem nothing surprising. The alienation of the English media from India's polity, and the solipsism and blindness of the elite it speaks for, are hardly anything new. Indeed, if anything 2004 was only a further exposé of what was already increasingly obvious.

But in a way this was precisely the reason why it was significant, for it hence had direct implications for the role that the English media has played in the rise of Indian neoliberalism. To discuss this role, it is first important to note that, in the absence of a political/institutional formation that has generated and defined Indian neoliberalism as an ideology (in contrast to Thatcherism, Reaganism, or other such forces), the effort to push neoliberalism as a political project in India has taken place in a far more diffuse and complex manner[1]. The functions that such a formation would play have, rather than being concentrated and organised, instead been dispersed to multiple centres of power in the Indian political system.

For instance, one such function—the individual policy changes and "reforms" that are required—has worked not through 'public opinion' or the legislative system, but instead through back door operations primarily focused in the bureaucracy (and, in cases that do require legislation, through "consensus" achieved by cross-party action through neoliberal elements without an organised formation). This was described by Rob Jenkins (1999) as a process of "reforms by stealth."

A second such role, increasingly appropriate in a time of shifts towards accumulation by dispossession (for which see below), has been played by the judiciary. This has been the elimination and dilution of, on the one hand, legal protections for labour and criminal procedure, and, on the other, the strengthening and widening of state coercive powers over resources (forests and urban lands being the two most striking examples).

But a third—and in our context most important—function has been the evolution and projection of a hegemonic ideological project for neoliberalism in the Indian context. And it is here, arguably, that the English media has played a very different role than merely being an arena for ideological debate. Instead, the English media—with some exceptions of course—have largely begun to behave like the direct ideological propagators of a distinctly neoliberal political project. Delusional reporting about economic growth and general prosperity, contemptuous dismissal of other points of view, and a strong shift towards "campaign-style" reporting are among the indicators of this. To choose three examples, it is now difficult to read "news" in the *Indian Express*, the *Times of India* or the *Hindustan Times* on any topical issue that is not brazenly pushing an agenda—and it is rare for that agenda to be anything other than the "national good" as defined by the neoliberal approach.

In this context one is reminded of Gramsci's (1971) remark 'the intellectual General Staff of the organic party often does not belong to any of these fractions, but operates as if it were a decisive force standing on its own... [one can think of] a newspaper too (or group of newspapers), a review... as a "party" or a "fraction of a party" or a "function of a particular party." ' Indeed, since 1991, far more than any political formation, the projection of the policy priorities of neoliberalism has taken place through this function of the English media.

Yet, over the period of the NDA regime, this diffuseness of the Indian neoliberal project began to coalesce around a deepening, albeit temporary, alliance with Hindutva and the Sangh Parivar. The synthesis of neoliberalism and Hindutva promoted by the NDA was articulated, adjusted and defined by the English media, operating as "organic intellectuals" of the ruling bloc[2]. The 'prediction' of the NDA's victory was both a 'factual' and a normative one; not only *should* the NDA win, it *obviously would* win because that was the natural outcome. Finally, "India Shining" was a remarkable melding of what was essentially a media strategy with an ideological vision that had already been articulated by the English media ad nauseam in the preceding years.

The Implications of Political Failure

In playing this role, however, the English media has not been serving as the intellectual "General Staff" or organic intellectuals of India's entire bourgeoisie. Rather, as the standard bearer of the neoliberal project, it has functioned as the intellectual vanguard of finance capital, the fraction that has driven the neoliberal agenda and that is, in that sense, largely the dominant fraction in India's ruling bloc.

But if one views the English media in this manner, the 2004 election defeat becomes not just an error in prediction, but a failure of an attempted political project. The fact that it was such a limited and partial defeat only increases the complexity of its implications. While there was no clarity on who or what actually led to the defeat, what was clear was that the hegemonic project being attempted had failed to *explain* India's political reality.

It is here that one returns to the function of hegemony in terms of *organising* the ruling class bloc. The function of the dominant bloc's intellectuals is not only to legitimise that dominance—it is to construct a vision of society that allows that bloc to understand its own dominance and to maintain it. What 2004 showed was that the ruling intelligentsia had not understood the sources of political power in Indian society. The result of the 2004 elections was thus a gap between the reality of continuing, if shaken, power for the dominant class fraction, and the inability of that power to devise an intellectual argument for itself.

The United "Progressive" Alliance: One Side of an Attempted Solution

One striking result of this disarticulation was to give the new UPA government a mild case of schizophrenia. The neoliberals retained and even strengthened their hold on traditional posts. Yet, simultaneously, the government initiated the process of preparing the CMP, which in turn became the basis for two new institutions: the National Advisory Council and the coordination committee with the Left parties. Neither the CMP process nor these new institutions reflected any major organised social interests; their direct political backing came only from the Left, whose support was a necessary but not sufficient condition for their activities. The importance of these institutions was not *political*, in the sense of state power, as much as*intellectual*. They were born out of the contradictory need to generate a new hegemonic project while simultaneously not affecting the interests of the ruling bloc and its dominant fraction, which after all remained in power (i.e. "reforms with a human face"). This institutional confusion in turn was the most apparent manifestation of the contradictions within the UPA's stumbling attempts towards a new ideological project.

It was this space that generated both the possibilities and

the limitations of the few progressive developments that did take place during the UPA's regime. Two of the UPA's flagship legislations are particularly good examples of the contradictions of this situation: the Employment Guarantee Act and the Forest Rights Act. Both laws challenged existing systems of state control in a significant manner, in the one case concerning finances and in the other on natural resources. Moreover, both laws were premised not on a process driven by state action, but one that both *presumed* and *sought to generate* popular action - in one case in the form of "employment on demand" and in the other through a gram sabha-based rights recognition process. Finally, both laws were pushed by informal alliances of local people's movements, progressive elements in the Congress and other parties, and the Left.

The threat that this posed to the 'old' neoliberal ideology was apparent from the uncannily similar opposition that these laws faced. In both cases an alliance formed against the Bills consisting of sections of the bureaucracy (the Ministry of Finance for the EGA and the Ministry of Environment and Forests for the forest rights bill), part of the English media and a handful of "experts" (some economists and wildlife conservationists respectively). The bureaucracies provided the basic argument, the experts justified it with theories varying from the legitimate to the totally irrational, and the press used both to mount a campaign against these measures. Further, the arguments themselves were almost identical. Both legislations were described as attempting "distribution of national resources" in "handouts" to "the poor" for the sake of "vote banks." Such "populist measures" would never bring "welfare" or "development" to the "beneficiaries", as they would be hijacked by "corruption". These measures would only keep people in "poverty" or "in the forests" instead of granting them a new and productive life (which in turn could only result from "growth"). In the process, the "nation" would be "immeasurably damaged."

The anxiety of a dominant social group facing a process of democratisation, however limited, is apparent in these arguments; and it was clear that in both cases, it was not the laws themselves so much as the possibility of democratisation that was seen as the threat. Yet, these two legislations—both of which would have been essentially inconceivable under the NDA—survived, albeit in a mangled form, and were eventually passed (to the point where, ironically, the very same EGA is now being hailed as a "stimulus" for tackling the financial crisis). Why did this happen?

One can speculate that the reason was precisely the peculiar 'radicalism' of these legislations. First, as noted above, neither represented a powerful or organised political interest, and were driven in large measure through loose, informal coalitions exploiting the space created by the UPA's "hegemonic vacuum". Second, while both did involve degrees of systemic change, they did so in a fashion that did not directly and obviously threaten the short-term interests of the ruling class fractions. Instead, as laws that depended entirely on popular mobilisation, they opened political spaces that could be used by democratic forces, but which dominant elements could also try to block (which is precisely what is happening with both laws at the present moment). These laws are thus less a measure of resource redistribution than they are an effort to change the locus of resource decision-making.

Yet such changes themselves are, in the long term, a threat to the neoliberal project—particularly in the Indian context, for reasons explored below. Those who could visualise, conceptualise and coordinate the response to such a long term threat—the organic intellectuals of the ruling bloc—did in fact attempt to do so, along with the more far-sighted members of the ruling class. But for the ruling bloc to fully respond to such challenges required a shared ideological approach, which was precisely what was in question. As a result, when no major fraction of the ruling bloc was directly threatened and all saw themselves as able to deflect these challenges, a constrained space opened for political action.

A similar pattern repeated itself in most of the other efforts by social forces to produce progressive results during the early years of the UPA. One can see the sharp contrast when such efforts did directly confront interests of ruling fractions—the alacrity with which the entire notion of private sector reservations was dispatched being a good example.

But this attempt at a "human face" was only part of the response to 2004, the part that indicated a transition in the function of the ruling intelligentsia. The other part, which built on tendencies that predated 2004, will arguably have a far greater impact.

The Other Response: The Use of Force

While 2004 is a convenient inflexion point for analytical purposes, it is clear that these processes did not begin in 2004. Indeed, as early as the late 1990s, it was already clear that the neoliberal political offensive was finding it increasingly difficult to devise a concrete coordination of interests that would allow its dominant fraction—finance capital—the full transformation of the Indian polity that it desires. This ultimately reflects the nature of India's political economy, and more proximately is a consequence of the lack of an organised institutional-political force (a party in the broad sense) pushing the Indian neoliberal project[3]. By this period, the financial press had begun to lament the inability to push through the remaining "big ticket" reforms, such as:

- Dismantling of labour laws;
- Withdrawal of food subsidies and withdrawal of the PDS;
- Privatisation of all major public sector enterprises;
- Withdrawal of fertiliser and other subsidies to agriculture;
- Complete liberalisation of FDI, particularly in sectors such as retail.

In each of these areas, utinroads, dilutions and sabotage have occurred, but the wholesale destruction of these regulatory and institutional mechanisms has not been achieved. Around this period, then, a shift began to occur away from reforms aimed at *deregulation* and towards reforms aimed at *expropriation*.

What does one mean by this? Since the late 1990s, the major

new initiatives in Indian neoliberalism have been in the area of what David Harvey (2003) described as "accumulation by dispossession" (or "accumulation by encroachment", in Prabhat Patnaik's (2005) terminology). This process, integral to capitalism at all times, is accentuated under neoliberalism, where both State assets and the assets of small commodity producers (such as peasants and artisans) become far easier to seize as a result of deflationary and 'rollback' policies. A classic instance is the huge increase in mining activity. As of 2006, the Orissa government had already signed two lakh crore worth of mining projects in the two years since the BJD-BJP regime's current term began. As of 2007, the Jharkhand government had over 54 Memoranda of Understanding for steel and power plants pending. Meanwhile, over five lakh hectares of forest land—at a rate three times higher than the preceding two decades—were diverted for various projects between 2001 and 2006, with much of this land being transferred for free to private companies. The number of industrial projects requiring state acquisition of land or resources has rapidly increased. Meanwhile, in addition to such direct use of state coercion, the collapse of credit for agriculture became a parallel process of intensifying extraction of resources.

In a sense this "strategy" has succeeded: between 2000 and 2005-06, the share of private corporate savings in total capital formation doubled from 6 to 12 per cent, and exceeded that of household savings for the first time (Chandrasekhar and Ghosh 2007). In the same period, corporate surplus rose from 12 to 16 per cent of national income. Meanwhile, the results of a *Business World* (2008) survey are indicative: before the financial crisis, seven of India's ten most profitable companies were either real estate or mining corporations.

The corporations that engaged in and promoted such strategies—Reliance, the Tatas, the Adanis, etc. come to mind —are in many ways precisely the dominant class fraction in Indian capital. By adopting such an approach, they had already begun a process of increasingly emphasising the moment of coercion within hegemony while de-emphasising the moment of consent. Reflecting the inability to produce a political project that would concretely coordinate their desire for super-profits with mass consent, they instead began to attempt to bypass resistance at the national and political level and to seek "short cuts" to more direct expropriation.

For instance, the most glaring example—state land acquisition for big projects—is a classic avenue of expropriation that does not require long term political support. Acquisition of this kind can operate on a short term, region-specific basis that does not require policy changes. Moreover, the subjects that most directly pertain to such strategies—land, water, forests, law and order, and so on—all either come only or mostly (forests) under the state governments. This, combined with the impoverishment of the States as a result of the Finance Commission awards and similar mechanisms, makes it much easier for corporates to simply demand and receive windfall profits through state action.

Before to 2004, this strategy was used in a relatively ad hoc manner on specific projects, even as its overall impact was increasingly visible in the crisis in agriculture. But the 2004 "defeat" of the neoliberal intelligentsia was a further reflection of the weakness of the neoliberal political project and, therefore, presumably increased the "attractiveness" of coercive expropriation.

Indeed, even as an attempt was being made to shape "reforms with a human face" under the UPA and the political schizophrenia noted above was underway, a simultaneous shift in the opposite direction was also taking place. The best indicator of this shift, and arguably the most politically significant "innovation" of this regime, is the 2005 SEZ Act. A close reading of this Act and Rules clearly indicates that these zones have little to do with exports and nothing to do with employment generation (their two most commonly cited justifications). Rather, they are an extreme version of the Chinese SEZ concept, wherein the entire state machinery of a territory is effectively handed over to private capital. Indeed, the *only* effective requirement for setting up an SEZ in India is possession (or even the possibility of possession, with state assistance) of sufficient land area. Within this area, in a brazen and unconstitutional manner, the law effectively creates an administrative machinery where the "Developer" corporate and a few agencies of the Central government are the sole governing, regulatory and economic authorities. Everything from public infrastructure to municipal governance is left to these institutions. The result is an ideal space for coercive, extractive accumulation by big capital with access to speculative finance, and indeed the Act's minimum land area stipulations are a particularly crude way of distinguishing between such capitals and smaller ones (much to the chagrin of smaller IT companies, for instance). The favoured neoliberal 'solution' to the resultant conflict is to allow for "market purchase of land", which not only fails to take into account the reality of land markets in India and does not address speculation through change of land use, but also ignores the fact that the possibilities for coercive accumulation are not limited to initial real estate speculation. The SEZs institutional systems ensure that these would include continued extraction of surplus from workers, smallholders and residents through the Developer's powers over infrastructure, security and land use, as well as large scale profiteering from subsidies and tax exemptions.

The SEZ Act thus effectively creates a legal and institutional structure for accumulation by dispossession, allowing it to be generalised beyond individual projects and corporates and made into a *regime* of accumulation accessible to big capital in general. Instead of attempting a neoliberal transformation of the state machinery as a whole, the Act creates a "shortcut" of extremely pro-capital institutions within defined small territories. This is effectively the *institutionalisation* of accumulation by dispossession as a strategy.

The SEZ Act was the most explicit manifestation of this political approach, but by the second half of the UPA government—from around 2006, for instance—it was clear that this had won the day against new efforts to devise a hegemonic ideology. Symbolised by the de facto dissolution of the NAC, and then later by a brazen embrace of US foreign policy, the dominant fraction of the ruling bloc appeared to have taken a final decision that the use of force and systematic "bypassing" of political institutions was more effective and more worthwhile than attempts at trying to win consent for its actions. This in turn was reflected in the collapse of practically all progressive statements and actions by the UPA. Even as they found the hegemonic fusion of neoliberalism and Hindutva in Gujarat under Narendra Modi to be ideal (symbolised by the sickening endorsement of Modi as the future Prime Minister), the Ambanis, the Mittals, the Tatas and their ilk had clearly decided that, if they cannot have that, immediate gains from robber baron expropriation are preferable to building consent.

Shadows of a Crisis

Yet this 'choice' is once again only a reflection of the growing fragility of the hegemonic project of this ruling bloc. For this is a self-interested, short term choice of the dominant fraction, a choice from which even smaller capitals—who cannot so easily utilise structures for accumulation by dispossession, and therefore face unfair competition—will not benefit. As a result, it will both exacerbate tensions within the ruling bloc as well as accelerate the trend towards an overall hegemonic crisis, with its attendant implications for the stability of domination by this fraction. A glaring instance is the SEZ Act's incredible tax exemptions, which constitute a resource transfer so huge that even ideological neoliberals in the Finance Ministry have found it difficult to stomach.

In the meantime, the global financial crisis is likely to have contradictory impacts. On the one hand it greatly weakens the dominant fraction and its strategy (as indicated by moves to get SEZs denotified). On the other, the neoliberals have sufficiently linked India's economy to international finance that the crisis has had significant and immediate negative impacts, both directly through rapid declines in export sectors and real estate/construction and indirectly through a sharp decline in international prices, particularly of agricultural produce (Ghosh 2009). This is only likely to produce further discontent and anger, accelerating a sense of hegemonic vacuum.

The shadows of the hegemonic crisis are already reflected in various aspects of the polity. At the formal political level, whereas 2004 was marked by a clear political project (the NDA's neoliberal-Hindutva synthesis) opposed by diffuse resistance, 2009 is marked by an open acknowledgment by all concerned—including the neoliberal media—that no political force can hope to secure a clear mandate. The fractious shifts within coalitions and resulting 'instability' reflect the lack of faith any political formation has in effectively deploying any hegemonic project, new or old.

At the level of popular struggle, the last four years have seen an expansion of new forms of popular action as well as more brutal types of repression. Some struggles, such as those of POSCO and Nandigram, declared de facto 'liberated zones', operated and controlled by direct 'people's power' institutions. Indeed it is no accident that three of the largest of such protests —Nandigram, Singur and Lalgarh—have taken place in West Bengal, a state where the hegemonic crisis is perhaps most acute, given the total swing to big capital by the Left Front government and the resulting collapse of space for dissent and resistance. These new forms of protest in turn reflect a lack of faith in more institutional forms of political action and a complete collapse of the legitimacy of the state. They show strong parallels to similar situations in Latin America (such as the Oaxaca Commune), where, too, a hegemonic crisis has resulted from a neoliberal offensive.

The response of the state has also, however, accelerated. Strategies once reserved for "peripheries" in Mizoram and Kashmir, such as state-sponsored militias and strategic hamleting, have found their place in the mainland with Salwa Judum. In Kashmir itself, the Israel-style massacres of protesters in August was on a level unprecedented since the early years of the uprising, and the confrontation all the more remarkable for the decision of the protesters to not engage in violence of any kind. Following the November Mumbai carnage, the UPA has also institutionalised—in the form of the National Investigative Agency and the reincarnated anti-terror laws—a new security infrastructure that will make repression more centralised, and possibly more intense.

Possibilities and Constraints

The fact that tendencies towards a crisis are present does not, of course, make it certain that the crisis will actually occur. What it does make clear, however, is that the Indian polity is in a fluid and complex situation where the boundaries of both conflict and possibility will be wider than before. The polity appears to be moving into a qualitatively new phase, and whatever resolution is eventually achieved, it will be most likely based on a broad reconfiguration.

This situation offers both challenges and possibilities to democratic and left forces. Firstly, the tendency towards coercive action by the state will greatly increase as the resort to force becomes more and more necessary to cover up fractures in hegemony. Secondly, a continued focus on accumulation by dispossession—if perhaps at a slower rate in the short term—will increase the number of people who are physically displaced, expropriated or forced to migrate. Such people have generally been much more difficult for left forces to organise.

Thirdly, the Sangh Parivar, while not capable of immediately offering a hegemonic project at the national level, is better organised, has a larger reach and has a more coherent political project than the scattered and fragmented left forces in the country. It also has the advantage of an inherent strong resonance between its project and the goals of the dominant fraction of the ruling bloc, reflected in the hegemonic alliance operating in Gujarat. Finally, displaced and otherwise mobile but disenfranchised groups have historically been a main target of Sangh organising. If we on the left do not act swiftly, one consequence of this fluid situation may be a rapid expansion and consolidation in the Sangh's strength.

But this should not blind us to the possibilities that exist in this situation. A hegemonic crisis is at the end of the day a product of the class struggle, a struggle that may not yet be consciously or coherently organised but which is driving the current situation. A hegemonic crisis offers the opportunity to push political positions that would otherwise be automatically excluded by hegemonic understanding. Since the ruling class is no longer "setting the agenda", we now have the space to move beyond defensive and reactive positions and to offer programmatic changes, even from a position of relative political weakness. To use Gramsci's terminology, this is a time when the war of position accelerates, even if one is not yet able to convert it into a war of manouvre. Even when one cannot confront the core interests of the ruling bloc, it is possible to occupy spaces and alter discourses more effectively now than perhaps at any time since the 1980s.

It is not a window we are likely to get often; and it is not one that we can afford to lose.

May 7, 2009

Notes

1. The reasons why such a formation does not exist is not something I am going into here. There is a partial discussion on this issue in Gopalakrishnan 2008.
2. Please see Gopalakrishnan 2006 for more discussion on this aspect.
3. This area is discussed more in Gopalakrishnan 2008.

Bibliography

Business World (2008). "Top 100 Most Profitable Companies", *Business World*. October 27.

Chandrasekhar, C.P. and Ghosh, Jayati (2007). "Who is Doing the Saving and Investing?", *Macroscan.org*, May 11.

Ghosh, Jayati (2009). "A Policy of Neglect", *Frontline*, January 31.

Gopalakrishnan, Shankar (2006). "Defining, Constructing and Policing a 'New India': Exploring the Relationship Between Neoliberalism and Hindutva", *Economic and Political Weekly*. Mumbai: Sameeksha Trust, June 30.

Gopalakrishnan, Shankar (2008). "Neoliberalism and Hindutva: Fascism, Free Markets and the Restructuring of Indian Capitalism", *Radical Notes Series*, Delhi: Aakar Books.

Gramsci, Antonio (1971). *Selections from the Prison Notebooks*. London: Lawrence and Wishart.

Harvey, David (2003). "New Imperialism: Accumulation By Dispossession," *Socialist Register 2004*, pp. 63-87.

Jenkins, Rob (1999). *Democratic Politics and Economic Reform in India*. Cambridge: Cambridge University Press.

Patnaik, Prabhat. (2005). "The Economics of the New Phase of Imperialism," *Macroscan.org*, August 26.

Poulantzas, Nicos (1978); tr. Camiller, Patrick. *State, Power, Socialism.* Paris: Presses Universitaires de France. Reprinted by Verso in 2000.

Yadav, Yogendra with Heath, Oliver and Kumar, Sanjay (1999). "The BJP's New Social Bloc", *Frontline.* Chennai: Kasturi and Co., November 19.

Yadav, Yogendra (2004). "The Elusive Mandate of 2004", *Economic and Political Weekly.* Mumbai: Sameeksha Trust, December 18.

8

The Unending Saga of Land Acquisition in West Bengal: When Enemies Make Strange Bedfellows

Anjan Chakrabarti

How should land be taken from the peasant for the process of urbanisation (real estate, infrastructural development, etc.) and industrialisation? This has remained one of the enduring questions in the West Bengal political scenario for the last few years. This is not surprising considering the fact that 'land acquisition' remains one of the indispensable conditions of existence for securing, facilitating and expanding capitalist organisation of surplus along industrial lines.[1] Henceforth if industrial capitalism is the goal, then 'land acquisition' as an issue is set to hog the limelight in the foreseeable future.

Two apparently contesting positions on land acquisition have correspondingly surfaced, one forwarded by CPI(M) and the other by the Trinamool Congress (TMC). The first argues that land be acquired directly by the state who then should deal with the developers while the second argues that it should be bought directly by the developers themselves. Interestingly, a third model of land acquisition has come to light in West Bengal whereby the state uses private agencies to acquire land from the farmers and then buy it back from those agencies for purposes it deems fit. This is the Vedic village model that caught negative attention with the case of land acquisition in the

Rajarhat area of West Bengal. Scanning the three models of land acquisition I argue that, for all their suggested differences, they provide diverse kinds of conditions of existence for creating and expanding capitalist organisation of surplus. In the process, the models of land acquisition for the purpose of industrial capitalism signal different routes for facilitating uniform development logic of transition from agrarian society to an industrial capitalist society. In contrast, I contend that the language of resistance against land acquisition in West Bengal with its refusal to comply with the centrality of industrial capitalism suggests the possibility of a different and perhaps fourth model. This suggested way though entails adopting a fundamentally alternative way to envisage the relationship between agriculture and industry as compared to the above mentioned three models; it also calls for rethinking the present model of top down governance that prevents people from exercising the power to take any effective decision and action regarding their lived social life.

Moreover, our discussion reveals that TMC's much vaunted model of land acquisition underlies a change in the strategy of ushering in industrial capitalism in West Bengal without in any manner contesting the logic of industrial capitalist development that one may argue was what the tumultuous protests against land acquisition in West Bengal signalled. That is, in proposing a switch from a state-sponsored land acquisition policy to a market-sponsored land acquisition policy, the TMC model calls for altering an important condition of existence for creating, securing and expanding the capitalist organisation of surplus. This is important to recognise because the much hyped 'MATI' slogan of TMC can be mistakenly misrecognised as a standpoint against the logic of capitalist industrial development. We want to argue here that nothing can be further from the truth. If its land acquisition policy is any indication, TMC's position, notwithstanding its 'pro-peasant' and 'pro-poor' rhetoric, would have the effect of charting a different strategy for securing the march of industrial capitalism at a time when the social movements have de facto put a halt to the current model of state-sponsored land acquisition. It is thus not accidental that the TMC including its supreme leader are now going all out to convince the industrial captains (the capitalists) about the effectiveness of its path and that its stance in no way represents an anti-industrialisation or anti-capitalist policy. Evidently, it does not. It is in fact favourably disposed towards them.

The First Model of Land Acquisition: State-Sponsored

This has been the dominant model of land acquisition in India thus far. The state directly acquires fragmented land from the peasants by compensating them or, as has happened in many cases, without doing so. Acquired land is reorganised into one or multiple bundles which are then marketed as exclusive and consolidated property to other state enterprises or to private agencies for their usage; the market for land acquisition is thus mediated by the state. Private land of the peasants and common property (land, resources, water, forest, etc.) are now turned into exclusive property of either state or private agencies.

With the advent of globalisation entailing the rapid expansion of private capitalist enterprises, this form of private-public partnership has deepened and gathered pace. It has almost become a norm for the state to acquire land for projects to be developed by private agencies. We can thus say that India in general and West Bengal in particular has been moving into a phase of consolidated privatisation of hitherto agricultural land in order to secure, facilitate and expand capitalist organisation of exploitation taking the material form of industrial expansion. It is not far-fetched to say that the state sponsored model of land acquisition qua consolidated private property bundles constitute an indispensable condition of existence for the current form of industrialisation process unfolding in India.

However, in recent times, this state sponsored model of land acquisition has come under serious questioning from the direct stakeholders, namely the peasants (a loose term encompassing different groups related to agrarian economy). As events in Kalinganagar, Nandigram, Singur and Raigarh, to mention only a few cases, exemplified the spirited resistance of the peasants and their supporting groups have put a spanner on the seemingly smooth process of this model of land acquisition forcing a rethinking on the part of Indian government. While the state governments did use a range of repressive apparatus in trying to break the back of these resistance movements, the following realisation has perhaps dawned on the concerned political establishment: state sponsored model of land acquisition without adequate compensation has become practically very difficult in the current democratic set up of India. One then has to somewhat change the model of land acquisition so as to secure and facilitate the goal of capitalist industrial development which evidently is taken as sacrosanct and beyond any questioning.

The Second Model of Land Acquisition: Marketisation

The Indian government has proposed to somewhat shift the process of land acquisition policy such that the government will secure a larger portion of land while the minority portion will be bought by the private agencies. While there are a host of regulatory mechanisms that have been proposed, one outstanding aspect is the assurance of adequate compensation (if not resettlement) in any land acquisition package. While concerned lobbies and political parties are haggling over the exact proportion of this private-public division and modalities of compensation, the Trinamool Congress has come out with another position.

In line with its 'MA, MATI, MANUSH' programme, TMC suggests that the state should in no way be involved in any acquisition of land. Land has to be obtained through the process of direct exchange between buyers (private or state agencies) and sellers (the farmers); unmediated market is the solution proposed by TMC. The implication is that the developers and/ or industrialists will have to buy the land directly from the farmers. Apparently, this model valorises ownership since it is the owner of land who will be legitimately accounted in the game of exchange. What remains unclear though is the status and predicament of other stakeholders related to land, say, for example, the agricultural workers. Will they be evicted without any kind of compensation? There are other deeper issues related to 'land acquisition' which we do not touch here.[2]

In this TMC model, it is not farfetched to imagine the emergence of a huge 'brokerage' land market in which 'land acquiring' private companies scout for land and try to create 'private land bank'. Once acquired and consolidated, they are then parcelled out in various proportions to industrial enterprises or some other agencies, public and private. Given the rapid pace of India's march towards industrial capitalism, TMC's model of land acquisition is bound to facilitate the emergence of such a kind of agrarian land market and its consequent 'private land bank'.

Does this solution impede the process of industrialisation and the associated capitalist organisation of surplus it helps create and expand? Hardly so, I contend. It simply modifies the land acquisition related condition of existence of capitalist organisation of surplus from state-sponsored to market-sponsored. Is the market solution a better solution for industrial capitalists in comparison to the state sponsored one? Which of the two processes of acquiring land is better for the farmers? Is a state-sponsored land bank better compared to a private land bank? Let us not address these important and topical questions here.

The Third Model of Land Acquisition: Public-Private Partnership

The third position stems from a mixture of the first and second. The first position concerns the motive of the state agencies to acquire land. This may be driven by the state's overall plan of development that entails paving the way for the expansion of capitalist organisation of surplus which though is currently made difficult by the state's inability to acquire land directly from the peasants. This inability can be mitigated by the second position involving the presence of unmediated market for land with buyers and sellers facing off one another. These two moments are telescoped in this way: as part of an overall plan of the capitalist led industrial development the state government outsources the process of buying land to an agency who then emerges as a genuine buyer in the market to acquire land directly from the peasants only to hand it over to the state government. Two kinds of contracts rule this model of land acquisition—a contract between state and private agency of land buyer and between the latter and the peasants. The former may take the form of a written or unwritten contract while the second has to be written and legally ratified. While this special kind of private-public partnership complicates the process of land acquisition, it has two advantages for the state: (i) it is able to wash its hands off the process of land acquisition even as it is able to get access to land, and (ii) it avoids getting directly implicated in any anomalies arising from the unmediated market process such as cheating on prices, fudging papers, arm twisting the sellers and so on. This is the Vedic Village Model and one can imagine multiple variations of my presented case.

Because the logic of the Vedic Village Model telescopes features of the first two models of land acquisition, it has quite ironically landed both CPI(M) and TMC in one line and made them strange bedfellows. On one side, CPI(M) became once again exposed on its development policy of favouring land acquisition (by whatever means it seems now) for industrial capitalists while TMC's cup of embarrassment is full when it became apparent that its policy of marketisation of land acquisition turned out to be the chief conduit for the state to acquire land and that too to fulfil the development agenda favoured by the CPI(M).

The Common Agenda of the Land Acquisition Models

Despite the differences between the land acquisition models, they exhibit a unified approach along the following lines:

(i) Openly or in silence, all the three models accept capitalist led industrial development as the motor of change and in that backdrop consider land acquisition as inevitable for the process of industrialisation. While the CPI(M) and Congress are unabashed about its need, TMC remains somewhat ambiguous in its rhetoric though its policy of land acquisition leaves us with no interpretation other than being favourably disposed towards capitalist industrial development. While TMC has firmly opposed state-sponsored land acquisition drive, it has not challenged land acquisition per se nor has it ruled out land acquisition for capitalist led industrial development. As such, if stretched to its limit, the different parties, for all their animosity, share the goal of industrial capitalist development. The difference boils down to the diverse strategies to be adopted to achieve that goal.

(ii) All the three models of land acquisition make sense only in the context of the following axiom: acceptance of the pre-given relations of verticality between a so-called forward looking industry and a backward looking agriculture leading to a top down development model of inexorable transition from agricultural society to an industrial society. Much as the TMC's rhetoric would imply otherwise, its model of land acquisition seems to be accepting of this axiom.

(iii) Moreover, all the positions share this common denominator: none have till now accepted delegating to the concerned people the power to say *no* to any proposed development projects which of course is tantamount to the rejection of the supremacy and inexorability of the logic of capitalist led industrial development. Of course, people may very well decide to prefer the option of saying *yes* to relocation and favour industrial development in that area; valorising agriculture and agrarian life is just as problematical as valorising industry and industrial life. Till now, the matter has been placed in a manner that presupposes an unambiguous *yes* to relocation, a rather mechanical presupposition that flows from the pre-determined logic of industrial capitalist development rather than from people's right of self-determination to say *yes* to relocation and industrial project. The issue is not fundamentally about whether people have the right to say *no* to dislocation or *yes* to relocation but instead it is whether one is able to exercise that right or not. It is a freedom that has no validity except in its realisation. If implemented, this freedom of exercising options reclaims what the logic of (capitalist) development has denied to these societies: effective choice to the kind of social life that people want to lead. In this context, the social movements we have been witness to testifies in no uncertain terms a fierce struggle in one axis: who will have effective control over social life in terms of decisions and actions. Internalising the ability to exercise the power to say no within any suggested policy paradigm would entail not only a shift in development policy. It would additionally radically alter the current organisation and constitution of policy making that hitherto has steadfastly retained its top down monarchist moorings which in turn operates by denying the people the required space for making choice including over the kind of social life they would want to lead. If the relevant conduits of exercising power to say *no* such as say through voting on development projects as in case of Raigarh in Maharashtra are not internalised within the land acquisition framework (which of course would resultantly drastically change too) then, no matter what we put on paper and what our intentions are, the power to say *no* remains in effect null and void in so far as the outcome is concerned. None of the land acquisition models that we know of internalises this option to exercise *no*.[3]

Vote Bank Relevance of 'MATI'

TMC's goal is clear. It is not to initiate a social revolution but to oust the CPI(M) from state power. Its politics is thus state centric in general and vote bank centric in particular. Correspondingly, it wants to control and limit any movements to serve its limited purpose. In this context, TMC has successfully carved out a place in West Bengal political space as the supposed champion of the people's struggles against the Left Front-sponsored policy of state-sponsored land acquisition which it used with good effect to break the grip of the CPI(M)'s dominance over the poor. I have discussed this in detail in another write up in *Radical Notes*.[4]

Despite this success through the highly advertised pro-poor re-positioning of the TMC, I am here suggesting that its proposed land acquisition policy and its claim of representing these peoples' struggles are contradictory in nature. The former I have argued suggests a pro-capitalist development model albeit through a different route while the latter indicates a rejection of the capitalist development model. How is TMC dealing with this contradiction? What is the role of its Land Acquisition model in this situation?

TMC led those movements which turned out to be directed *against the state* which incidentally is ruled by the CPI(M) led Left Front. Against its stated objective of ousting the CPI(M) from state power, this strategy is understandable because after all it was the CPI(M) which came to personify this state sponsored model of land acquisition. A first glance at all these social movements might suggest that people rejected state sponsored drive towards industrialisation. That is indeed true and the TMC's success lay in cultivating and encapsulating this spirit of the social movements within its political slogan of 'MATI'.

However, such an analysis when made has limited value that, if deemed as absolute and final, is perhaps purposefully done to incarcerate and circumscribe the language and aspiration of the movements. Obsession with state-sponsored land acquisition obfuscates a deeper question that lay clearly at the heart of these movements. It pertains to the fact that the people were not just saying no to state-sponsored land acquisition but to the very idea of giving up land and their forms of life for ensuring the march of industrial capitalism, a change which as it was proposed stood as something alien to their existence and hence summarily rejected. It was the very idea of land acquisition for industrial capitalism that is the bone of contention here; it was also about the process of acquiring land (the governance question) which surfaced as a question through the movements. One can read the social movements as signalling not a rejection of the form (state-sponsored land acquisition) but the content (of land acquisition per se for industrial capitalism) itself. That is, the act of saying no to state-sponsored development telescoped an aspiration and demand to have the power to say no to the idea of development as projected in the model of inexorable transition from agrarian society to an industrial society that, by its very logic, is supposed to be beyond any contestation.

Read in this light, TMC's political strategy becomes evident: it is advertising the form as the content and in doing so trying to occult any proposed struggle over the content from the political space. That is, in its first stage, it wrapped the CPI(M) into its critique of a state-sponsored model that captured the voice of the people's immediate demand and now in its second stage is proposing a political solution calling for the replacement of CPI(M) with TMC so that this state-sponsored land acquisition policy is rendered obsolete. However, its own alternative on the issue of land acquisition suggests that this in no way is a contestation of the content, that is, land acquisition furthering the logic of capitalist induced industrialisation process. Rather, it implies a change in strategy for enacting industrial capitalism in West Bengal that would involve a policy change in land acquisition from model 1 to models 2 and/or 3. Put bluntly, TMC's model remains an apology of capitalist industrial development with its underlying relation of verticality between industry and agriculture that is based on a deeper logic of a devalued agriculture giving way to industrial society. No matter what it says on the contrary, its second model of 'marketisation of land' or the third model of 'public-private partnership model of Vedic village' can't lead us to any other explanations than my suggested one.

This clearly reflects TMC's vote bank strategy of ousting CPI(M) from state power. After all, state-based politics is about winning control of the state through elections. If its declared objective is limited to defeating CPI(M) in that plane, then it is rational for TMC to limit its political programme to winning that control over the body of state. The CPI(M) made the blunder of its lifetime by aligning itself with a policy of state-sponsored land acquisition that was rejected by the people through social movements. Having successfully clubbed the CPI(M) with this highly unpopular state-sponsored land acquisition policy TMC can now dream of fulfilling its objective of capturing state power. This is fine as far as it goes. However, those who are looking for any 'revolutionary' content in TMC need to take a step back from its rhetoric and give a quieter and deeper look at its actual policy of land acquisition. That policy is not only bent on occulting the content of social movement against land acquisition for industrial capitalism but by subsuming the content into the form it is veering towards obfuscating, wittingly or unwittingly, the 'revolutionary' content of the social movements as a whole. TMC's 'Leftism' stumbles and falters in the face of this observation and the limitation of 'MATI' as symbolising the 'pro-poor' and peasant-friendly face of TMC starts becoming palpable.

Conclusion

Did the social movements against land acquisition imply a case for stasis? We don't quite see it that way. At the minimum, we see these as packing a call to rethink and drop the idea of development from its moorings in a big bang shift that is top down and as if inexorably proceeding from a dismantling of agrarian society towards the creation of an industrial society. In contrast, these social movements perhaps encapsulate an aspiration to rethink development as an idea of community building (constituting both agricultural and industrial endeavours) rather than community destruction. They also signal a rejection of top down control and governance of peoples' social life whereby the people are excluded from making effective choices regarding the trajectory of their social life. Set against this background, TMC's effort to mask the contradiction with the help of its 'pro-poor' rhetoric that is at the same time supported by a land acquisition policy which tries to circumscribe the scope of the social movements against land acquisition within a simplified movement against state-sponsored model of land acquisition has its limitations. This is because the contradiction involving the people's demand for control of their social life, including economic life, that involves a rejection of the inexorable logic of industrial capitalist development and that of a land acquisition policy (model 2 and

3) favouring industrial capitalist development is real and not going to fade away any time soon. Given that all sides are, notwithstanding their different routes, favourably disposed towards industrial capitalist development in West Bengal, the schism between the suggested policies of the political elite (no matter their diverse forms) and those demanded by the social movements would guarantee the persistence of the question of land acquisition in the body politic of West Bengal in the foreseeable future. Change in state power from the CPI(M) to TMC that at this moment looks likely will not settle this issue any time soon.

October 5, 2009

Notes

1. By capitalist organisation of surplus we mean the process through which capitalists appropriate and distribute the performed surplus labour of the workers. Different economic, cultural, political and natural processes provide diverse conditions of existence for this process of surplus labour to be performed, appropriated, distributed and received which following Resnick and Wolff (*Knowledge and Class: A Critique of the Political Economy,* Chicago University Press, 1987) we name as class. Class therefore refers to processes relating to a particular form of performance, appropriation, distribution and receipt of surplus labour. While numerous organisations of class processes (capitalist, feudal, slave, independent, communist, communitic) coexist in an economy, our focus in this paper remains capitalist class process or capitalist organisation of surplus. Depending upon the effects from varied conditions of existence, the capitalist organisation of surplus emerges in diverse forms across time and space; just as the changing capitalist organisation of surplus will constitute the condition providing processes; class and non-class processes overdetermine one another and impacted by their contradictory influences and effects on one another the processes tend to procreate or wither in a never ending state of flux. 'Land acquisition' is one such condition of existence whose varied forms will have its constitutive effect on the kind of capitalist organisation of surplus that will emerge; similarly the changing capitalist organisation of surplus, say, resulting from globalisation and increased competition, has greatly impacted

the nature of 'land acquisition' and the debate occurring with respect to it. For an analysis of transition and development in India from a class focused overdeterminist perspective, see Anjan Chakrabarti and Stephen Cullenberg (*Transition and Development in India,* Routledge, 2003), and for an account of land acquisition and dislocation see Anjan Chakrabarti and Anup Dhar (*Dislocation and Resettlement in Development: From Third World to World of the Third,* Routledge, 2009).

2. See Anjan Chakrabarti and Anup Dhar (*Dislocation and Resettlement in Development: From Third World to World of the Third,* Routledge, 2009) for details.
3. See Anjan Chakrabarti and Anup Dhar (*Dislocation and Resettlement in Development: From Third World to World of the Third,* Routledge, 2009) for details of this alternative way.
4. Anjan Chakrabarti. 'The Return of the Repressed: Explanation of the Left Front Defeat in West Bengal'. Thursday, May 21, 2009, *Radical Notes* (reproduced as Chapter 5 in this book).

9

Forest Areas, Political Economy and the "Left Progressive Line" on Operation Green Hunt

Shankar Gopalakrishnan

As central India's forest belts are swept into an ever-intensifying state offensive and resulting civil war, there has been a strong convergence of left, liberal and progressive arguments on Operation Green Hunt. This note argues that this 'basic line' is problematic. The line can be summarised as:

- The conflict is rooted in resource grabbing by corporate capital, in the form of large projects, SEZs, mining, etc.
- Such resource grabbing leads people to take up arms to defend themselves, resulting in the ongoing conflict.
- The conflict thus consists of a state drive to grab people's homes and resources, with people resisting by taking to arms as self-defence.

Supporters of the Maoists' positions now often conflate these points with the more orthodox positions on the necessity for "protracted people's war" in a 'semi-feudal semi-colonial' state. Liberals in turn tend to deny these orthodox positions and instead advocate the resource grab—displacement—corporate attack issue as the "real" explanation. Both, however, accept this as the predominant dynamic at the heart of the current conflict.

But at the heart of this line lies an unstated question: why are forest areas the main battleground in this war? While the conflict is not coterminous with the forests—most of India's forest areas are not part of this war, and the conflict extends outside the forest areas in some regions—forests are both politically and geographically at its heart.

Most answers to this question are either over-specific—"the minerals are found there"—or over-general—"these areas are backward/remote/marginalised, a creation of uneven development, and the state is weak there." The latter are all correct generalisations, but in themselves they beg the question: why are these areas backward, marginalised and under-developed? This note argues that we need to engage with the political economy of forests and the nature of accumulation in these belts before we can accurately answer this question. Such an engagement, in turn, reveals political risks in the standard narrative.

The Forest Areas

Some basic features of the political economy of forest areas are outlined in a sketch here. The key defining feature of these areas is one legal-political-institutional complex: India's system of forest management. The British initiated the current system of resource control in forest areas in the mid 19th century, and it reached its present form around the turn of the 20th century. The system has since then maintained a remarkable continuity for more than a century, an indicator of its importance to India's ruling classes.

This system has its roots in the requirements of British industrial capitalism in the nineteenth century, for which timber was a key raw material, both within India (for the railway networks that strengthened imperial control and allowed extraction of resources) and in the UK itself (particularly ship building). The systems of forest control that existed in India at the time, where village communities, religious institutions, local rulers and tribal societies operated multiple and complex systems of management, did not permit such easy extraction. They also did not serve British interests, since timber trees were naturally not given high priority in such management systems. As a result, the British instituted the Forest Department and passed a series of three Forest Acts—in 1865, 1878 and 1927—to essentially bring India's timber resources under their control and provide a legal-institutional form for their management. The 1927 Act remains India's main forest law.

The British Forest Acts were based on the principle of expropriation: any area could be declared to be a government forest, whereupon rights in this area would have to be respected/settled (the process varied over the course of the three acts). The form of such rights was whittled down to essentially individual land rights by the time of the 1927 law, and even these were subject to the decision of a forest settlement officer. The resulting failure to record even the individual rights of adivasis, Dalits and most other forest dwelling communities is well documented. This process continued and was consolidated after independence, except in the Northeast.

But this was not merely a question of administrative failure. The forest laws had *three key consequences for production relations*. The first was that, as with enclosures anywhere, they sought to reduce what were essentially territories and landscapes to commodities, in this case exemplified by timber. The variations in pre-colonial management systems notwithstanding, none of them was based on principles of commodity management; though often far from democratic or egalitarian, they were concerned with regulation of use and (at most) extraction of revenue. Their purpose did not revolve around the extraction of a single commodity; this was an innovation of the British. The result of this process was to bring Indian forests into a specific position within the global capitalist commodity circuit, servicing the industrial needs of transport sectors within the imperialist bourgeosie.

But, unlike the classical enclosures of England, in the enclosure attempt in India's forests failed—bringing about the second consequence. The attempt to seize most of central India's forests met with fierce resistance, being one of the triggers for a series of adivasi uprisings across central India (the tribals of the Northeast having largely fought off British control from the beginning). The British lacked the force to clear these areas of people and suppress their management systems, and the post colonial Indian state—despite its ever increasing reserves of repressive power—has also lacked the ability to do so. The result has been that one reality exists in the world of law, where forests are uninhabited wilderness, and another exists in reality, where millions use and depend on them for survival. More important than the fact that these uses are illegal is that they are not recorded, and as such outside the *knowledge* of the state system.

This produced the third and most important consequence: a distorted system of property relations, from the point of view of classical 'capitalism'. In short, security of private tenure does not exist in the forests. Enclosure, rather than creating and defining the rule of private property, has produced a chaotic situation of competing claims, *de facto* management systems that clash with *de jure* ones and state policies that are based on a combination of fantasy at the time of policymaking (Project Tiger, for instance) and brutality in implementation. These apply to all resources in the area, not only to land.

Integration into India's Political Economy

A lack of defined property relations has, in turn, further shaped both the integration of these areas into Indian capitalism[1] and the forms of resistance adopted by people in these areas. First, *accumulation in these areas is simultaneously constrained and driven by the direct exercise of state force*. Close relations with the formal state machinery are a precondition for acccumulation in forest areas, whether one is a tendu leaf contractor, a landlord, a tea estate, a forest guard or Vedanta. This is accumulation by dispossession as a continuous process.

Such a situation obviously poses risks both to legitimacy and to 'orderly' accumulation. But it also proves to be a useful compromise in a context where state force alone simply cannot exterminate or remove the entire forest dwelling population. The current situation provides direct benefits to large sectors of India's ruling classes. On the one hand, the continuous subsidy to capital that is created by the provision of free or cheap minerals, water, timber and land from forest areas has contributed an untold and inestimable amount to India's capitalist 'development', both earlier and in the recent neoliberal era. It is no accident that most large projects at all stages since independence have involved forest land. On the other hand, this situation has produced a partially proletarianised population of crores of people—mostly, but not only, adivasis—whose traditional productive resources (particularly forest produce) have been expropriated, and who are now vulnerable to super-exploitation as migrant workers. Nor are the consequences limited to present-day forest dwellers; the resulting desperate reserve army of workers has had a historical and geographical 'ripple effect', diminishing the strength of the working class as a whole (most visible in the heavy and increasing use of adivasi migrant labour across India's "developed" capitalist belts).

Resistance in Forest Areas

The consequence of this is that the link between capital, the state and the use of force is thus blatantly obvious in forest areas in a manner that it is not elsewhere. If hegemony consists of the combination of consent with the armour of coercion, it is the armour that forest dwellers see. This, together with the reality of ill-defined property relations, has had consequences for the way people have fought back.

Indeed, I would argue that *the persistence and reproduction of collective property relations among adivasi and tribal communities is not the result of some kind of historical exceptionalism, or relics of a "past culture" or "feudal mode of production."* Rather they are a reflection of the concrete combination of weak private property relations and state repression on the other. In the forest and tribal areas, the *nature* of capitalist exploitation makes collective production both concretely possible and a key source of resistance (since it is the subject of direct repression), and as a result these forms of production are being reproduced. Indeed, the communities with the strongest systems of collective production in India today are the tribal communities of the Northeast, such as the Nagas, the Mizos, the Garos and others, who have literally been at war against expropriation attempts continuously since the colonial period. In central India, where such struggles have been less successful, the state suppression of community management systems has progressed much further—but they remain alive in such phenomena as community forest management (practised by thousands of villages in Orissa and Jharkhand), collective gathering and management of minor forest produce, collective grazing systems, etc.

Where internal differentiation has occurred, as it has in all communities, such differentiation has also been 'distorted'. It has produced small elites, generally among those close to the state machinery (including beneficiaries of reservations, panchayat leaders, JFM Committee members, etc.), who are polarised against large masses of people on the brink of destitution. This is also true among non-adivasi forest dwelling communities, most of whom were already integrated into a greater degree of private property relations before the declaration of state forests, but among whom similar processes have operated in forest areas.

Forms of Resistance

The net result of this has been to produce a situation where the state is both strong and weak. The strength, of course, stems from the availability of force and the lack of integration into the mainstream political system, which ensures that any agitation is met with inhuman repression. But the weakness stems from the lack of hegemony and the very clear boundary between "rulers" and "ruled." In the forest areas, the binary of "state vs people" has a glaring reality that people experience in their daily lives. The state both is and is seen to be the direct agent of exploitation.

The result is that struggles in these areas have often given space for more radical formations, and for raising more fundamental political issues, than in other parts of India. This is not just true of the CPI(Maoist), but of the history of struggles in adivasi areas generally, both before and after independence. Often phrased in millenarian and revivalist language, the adivasi uprisings of the 19th century demanded not just the exit of the

British but the reconstruction of their entire society. Closer to the present day, the undivided CPI found some of its strongest bases among adivasis, as have both the CPI (Maoist) and the democratic mass organisations. The longest running armed conflicts in India—the struggles in the Northeast—are also marked by the same dynamics. Meanwhile, the weakness of the state has also made it the target of other struggles in forest areas. For instance, practically all streams of the Indian left—from the parliamentary parties through the armed groups and the mass organisations—have staged their most successful drives for land occupation (i.e. land takeovers by the landless) on forest land.

Forests and the War

It is incorrect, in this light, to see forests as either *separate* from Indian capitalism or society or to see them as simply the more *remote or backward* parts of that society. Rather, forests and forest areas function within a specific politico-economic space *as a result* of the manner in which they are integrated with the Indian economy. It is not that there are no similarities between this space and that of other parts of the Indian socio-economic formation; there are parallels with the role of the state in urban areas, for instance, or with the nature of oppression among the landless peasantry. But the specificity of forest areas, produced by their role within the current socio-economic formation, is still valid. As said earlier, most of the current discussion on Operation Green Hunt does not recognise this fact, and instead seeks to both over-specify it and, more importantly, over generalise it.

The tendency to over-specify is visible in a factual error made by nearly all current cirtiques: the argument that the conflict is over corporate projects. Displacement by corporations and projects covers a huge area in absolute terms, but this is only a small part of India's forests and adivasi areas. The vast majority of adivasis and forest dwellers, including in Maoist areas, are not threatened with displacement, and will not be threatened with it, however intense the corporate offensive may become.

To fail to see this is to open an obvious factual contradiction that is easy for the state and its supporters to attack. If the armed struggle is a question of self-defence against displacement, the Digvijay Singhs immediately ask why the CPI(Maoist) did not so strongly oppose displacement-inducing projects earlier. Others demand to know that if the only issue is corporate projects, why are some of the most intense struggles being fought where there is no project visible? Moreover, say the news anchors, if the war is one of self-defence against corporate displacement (which after all does not apply to most of India), is the CPI(Maoist) being delusional when it talks of overthrowing the Indian state? Indeed, by over-emphasising the displacement issue, many reduce the Maoist movement to precisely the kind of formation that they are most critical of: an issue-based anti-displacement struggle, with all its ideological and political vulnerabilities.

The answer to all these questions, of course, is that the struggles (armed and unarmed) in forest areas are not a response to displacement alone; they are a result of the continuum of state-driven repression and expropriation that dominates in these areas, of which corporate projects are but the most extreme example. Operation Green Hunt may have been initiated due to corporate pressure, but the war as a whole is much older and much broader.

But to accept this is to, in turn, open another flank for attack. If displacement and "annihilation" are not the issue, can it be said that there is "no choice" but to take up arms? If oppression in the forests is the problem, many mass organisations have worked in these areas before the Maoists, and many such struggles continue both there and elsewhere. True, most of these organisations have resorted to physical self-protection when attacked—the vast majority were and are not Gandhians. But there is a gulf between such "violence" and the strategy of protracted people's war.

In order to respond to this, many abandon over-specific arguments, but instead fall into over-generalisation—using simplified versions of traditional Maoist positions. In this view, the war in the forests is the "leading edge" of working class struggles in the country, a result of the intensification of "neo robber baron capitalism"[2]. This war is here presented as the most radical response to a brutal state intent on expropriating everything from its oppressed, and the rest of India's working class should, in this view, look upon the war as both model and inspiration. The CPI(Maoist) itself tends to adopt this position in its recent public statements (being clear, after all, that it is not fighting an anti-displacement struggle).

But it is not clear how a struggle that currently has its deepest roots in forest areas - with their specific history—can be described as the "leading edge" of a new democratic revolution. There is no linear manner in which the forest areas can be placed on a continuum of backwardness from the other areas of India; their configuration is specific to them, with some similarities but many differences with formations in other parts of the country. Sweeping claims of being a "leading edge" would only be true if the war in the forests is obviously generalisable, in the sense of developing a praxis that is extendable to other areas and configurations of exploitation in the country. This is not clear in either Maoist statements or in the external analyses that adopt this line.

Indeed, one might note, as a "stylised fact", that in some senses the Maoist organisations have undergone the opposite journey—from having their core base among sectors of the landless and the marginal peasantry, who are more within 'normal' state functioning and property relations, their centre has moved into the forest areas. Even within the forests, the majority of communities and areas are not within the Maoist fold. The party has shown less ability to expand in regions such as western Maharashtra, south Gujarat, western Madhya Pradesh, etc., where—owing to regional social processes and struggles—the forest economy has shifted more towards a "normal" peasant configuration. Thus, overall, the party appears to have moved from areas of stronger hegemony to ones of weaker hegemony. This does not strengthen belief in the ability of "people's war", as they frame it, to be a strategy of struggle in areas where binary "state vs people" modes of exploitation do not exist so concretely.

And it is here that the more fundamental danger arises. Posing the question of people's war as an inevitability, a choice between a marauding state intent on annihilating people and a revolutionary force whose promise lies in making a "better state", does not correspond to the political reality of most of the oppressed in India today. For all its venality, brutality and inhumanity, the Indian state retains a weakened but still very real hegemonic status in most of the country. For most working class Indians, bourgeois democracy may have *failed* to deliver its claims, but it is not a lie; and to merely declare that it is one is not going to make it so.

To ignore this, and focus only on the state's coercive operations in the forests, makes the conflict appear either irrelevant or, worse, alien to the majority of the population. It converts oppression rooted in Indian capitalism into the problem of some remote distant area, a war between "tribals" and "corporates" in what seems to be a foreign land. This, ultimately, only serves the government's purposes; what better way to ensure that opposition to Operation Green Hunt, outside the conflict zones, fails to develop a mass character? Instead of weakening state hegemony, we thus find ourselves reinforcing it.

Alternative Possibilities

If we are to place Operation Green Hunt accurately within our own analyses, it is important to stress the *connections* and *parallels* between the forest conflict and oppression in other areas, without slipping into over-generalisations. These parallels operate at different levels. One instance is the increasing use of law as a direct tool of accumulation, such as through Special Economic Zones, anti-encroachment drives in urban areas, etc. There are strong similarities between these processes and the use of forest law; exposing this function of law in turn exposes the class nature of the state. Another similarity is the continuous process of enclosure and extermination of systems of common production, often using the law, but also through other methods.

Which parallels are relevant and how are, of course, matters of separate debate. In this of course there will be sharp differences with the various left streams on our understanding of the present socio-economic formation. In general, however, such connections need to be exposed and analysed to build both a broader praxis and an understanding of how, in each sphere of struggle, hegemony can be weakened. But to simply overlook the political positioning of forest areas and continue with over-specific or over-general arguments is to risk strengthening the government's narrative—with attendant dangerous consequences for us all.

May 30, 2010

Notes

1. In this note, I am not entering into the debate as to whether this is genuine autonomous capitalist development or that of a compradore bourgeoisie; for the limited purpose here, there is little difference.
2. An example of the former is Saroj Giri, "'The Dangers Are Great, the Possibilities Immense': The Ongoing Political Struggle in India"; for the latter see Bernard D'Mello, "Spring Thunder Anew".

List of Contributors

Deepankar Basu teaches Economics at the University of Massachusetts, Amherst.

Pranab Kanti Basu teaches Economics at Vishwa-Bharati.

Anjan Chakrabarti teaches Economics at the University of Calcutta.

Pratyush Chandra is associated with *Radical Notes*.

Pothik Ghosh is associated with *Radical Notes*.

Shankar Gopalakrishnan is an activist of the *Campaign for Survival and Dignity*.